It Was Worth It All

By

ELLY MATZ

End-Time Handmaidens, Inc.
Engeltal
P. O. Box 447
Jasper, Ark. 72641

FOREWORD

It has been a deeply moving experience for me to work with Elly Matz on the story of her life. I feel unworthy to "touch the hem" of this twentieth century pilgrim whom God sent to us from the land of suffering.

As you read this story, I pray that God will give you a great compassion for Russia and the beautiful people who yet remain buried all the way from the frozen Arctic to the sunny Crimea.

The part of the country that Elly came from is not far from the area where my forefathers lived. They were Germans also.

As you follow her wanderings you will often be moved to tears. Offer each tear up to Jesus on behalf of those who are left behind—the mothers and fathers and sisters and brothers whom we will never meet until we stand on heaven's golden streets. We will understand it all so much better then and everyone of us will say with Elly, *"It was worth it all!"*

—Gwen Shaw

* * *

Elly Matz is available for speaking engagements. Please write to her, c/o End-Time Handmaidens, P. O. Box 447, Jasper, Arkansas 72641.

PREFACE

For many years the story of my life lay hidden deep in my subconscious. I had seen so much suffering, not only in my life, but the lives of my people, that I never wanted to remember it again. This caused me much mental agony and, even though I was in America, the land of my dreams, I continued to suffer.

Then one day I went to a home prayer meeting and I heard the testimony of another young woman who, like myself, had come from behind the Iron Curtain. Sigi spoke on the subject, *"Agree With Your Adversary."** It was as if God was talking to me through her. He began to break the seal over my entire emotions. I felt like screaming, "Stop her!" I wanted to run out of the room, but it seemed like the Lord held me down on the chair and said, "No, you've got to face it. I want to heal you!" And as Sigi walked over to me and began to pray for me, my memories were healed. Only because of that can I tell the truth.

My heart is burdened for America as I see her following in the footsteps of compromise with evil like my national leaders did in Russia over sixty years ago. I know that if we do not humble ourselves and repent, the Red Army could soon be marching in our city streets. Only the righteousness of the nation can save her. This end-time battle is not one of Communism vs. Capitalism, or Russia vs. America, but the powers of evil against the holiness of God.

I pray that my story will help to wake up the nation and the people whom I have loved since childhood. If God can use this testimony to do that, then I know that every pain I suffered, every grave I dug, every loved one I lost, every tear I shed will be worth it all. —Elly Matz

---

*AGREE WITH YOUR ADVERSARY, a soul-stirring, life-changing Bible study by Sigi, can be ordered from the End-Time Handmaidens for $2.00 postpaid. The tape to go with it is $4.00 postpaid

Chapter 1

A DREAM FULFILLED

Long before I came to the United States I loved this country, its people, its customs, its history and even its motto, "In God We Trust." I arrived in New Orleans in 1952, twenty-six years after I professed at the age of six that I would some day go to America. In those many years there were times when it looked absolutely impossible that I would achieve my dream, but there was a hope that flickered like a candle deep within my being that urged me to press on and on. No matter what bizarre circumstances placed me in foreign countries—Poland, Czechoslovakia, Germany—after I left my homeland of Ukraine, Russia, I knew these places were temporary, for I was not at peace as long as my fantasies revolved around that far-off land of America.

I shall never forget that day as the army ammunition ship, "The General Sturgis," sailed into the port of entry at New Orleans. Two thousand immigrants from every nation were packed into that green military ship — Jews, Russians Germans, Poles, Czechs, Hungarians, etc. As we entered the harbor, the only sight that caught and held my eye was the flag of stars and stripes that floated in the heavens above. Oh, how my heart leapt, for now my dream was a reality! I was "home" at last! The flag seemed to fly for me alone and as high as that flag was, so were my hopes that day.

We were soon led to a large harbor building which resembled a barn and were told to sit down and await further instructions. I was accustomed to waiting, so that did not faze me. It had taken nine months to process my family's papers in Munich, Germany, so what were a few hours more? I was told that my sponsor, Msgr. Thomas J. O'Dwyer of Los

1

Angeles, California, did not come for us for various reasons. And so we sat, my husband Alex, my thirteen-year-old son, Arnold, and my small boy of two-and-one-half years, Lennie. We sat and we sat. One by one everyone's name was called out, until only our family remained.

I approached the desk, not knowing how I would communicate. I spoke Russian, German and Polish and hoped to find someone who could speak one of these languages. A person who processed the immigrants asked in Yugoslavian what language I spoke. Since many words are common, I was able to communicate some. She informed me that my sponsor in Los Angeles had not been able to hold the apartment and the job he had promised us due to the delay we had had in Germany, so we couldn't be accepted in California. We were to be placed on a train for a two-day trip to New York and would report to the N.C.W.C. (National Catholic Welfare Conference) on Madison Avenue. Someone would meet us at Grand Central Station. I suppose one might despair, lose hope, or at least be disappointed by this reception in a new country, but I was not shaken in the least. Everything seemed like an adventure at the time.

As we rode through the country on the train, everything seemed enormous, beautiful and with unlimited possibilities. As we passed through one station after another and followed the tracks from city to city, we saw the vast greatness of America. As the landscape stretched and widened on each side of the track, so my heart widened with boundless love for this country. My family and I were like little children trusting in God's guidance, even though we never expressed it to one another. Stripped of language, money, possessions and in a new country, we had only the Lord in whom we could trust. Philippians 4:19, "God will fulfill all your needs." And thus far, we had been cared for and guided.

Remembering

While riding along I could not help but think of how

many long years and how far a journey I had traveled to be here at last. As the cars, houses, cattle and fields whizzed past, I thought back to where it all began—South Ukraine, Russia—my childhood, my mother, my father, my brother and sisters and my babushka (grandmother) whom I had loved so dearly. She was my father's step-mother and she had four children by a previous marriage but her big heart always had room for all the children in the family. How did this adventure begin? It had all begun with stories told us by my father. I could visualize myself as a little child of six, when my father held me on his lap and told stories on the long, cold winter nights. How secure we felt then! The fires burned brightly in the fireplaces at either end of the kitchen. The burning wood crackled occasionally but its sound was comforting like the purring of a kitten to a little child. Mother and Grandma were weaving and knitting. They were always busy making clothes for the family. We children were sitting and listening as father told stories about other countries and other lands. He often told about a great (powerful) country far across the land and seas . . . America. And as he told these tales, my heart caught fire whenever he would speak of the United States. I became so caught up with desire to go there, that one night I could contain myself no longer. I stood up and announced, "When I grow up I'll go to the United States." It wasn't really a prayer, it was a desire finally spoken aloud. And yet I know God heard me. Psalm 38:9 tells us, "Lord, all that I long for is known to you."

From that moment on I was a fanatic about going to America. Babushka would ask me, "What will you be when you grow up?" I would always answer, "I'm going to the United States." I said it so often and to so many people, they soon began to think I was crazy. "How can you go to the United States? The borders are closed," they would say. But still I persisted. Once a boy named Jacob asked me where I got my new felt boots. I said confidently, "From America!" (They weren't, of course.) In my mind I wasn't even living in Russia. In my desires and dreams I was already living in the

3

United States. Once the G.P.U. (local Russian secret police) came to ask my father what our connection with America was. Father was startled by their arrival at our door; and when they left he rebuked me for telling these stories. But, as a child, I really believed them, for in my mind I was already living in America. Hebrews 11:1 says: "To have faith is to be sure of the things we hope for, to be certain of the things we cannot see."

I learned at an early age that we were not to speak of the Lord, our God, at all. When Stalin came into power, our churches were burned down and crosses were destroyed, no matter where they were found. Because of the many crosses on the graves, even our cemeteries were desecrated and then plowed under. In school we were indoctrinated with the idea that God did not exist and that religion was an opiate for the mind. As children, we had to be very careful not to speak of prayer or what was seen or said in our homes. But my family did pray. Babushka would make us pray at a certain time in the morning and evening. Yes, I can even remember that at 12:00 noon we would say the Angelus—"The angel of the Lord declared unto Mary that she had conceived of the Holy Spirit, and the Word was made flesh and dwelt amongst us." I know now why Babushka would insist on a certain time to pray, for it formed a habit in us. Yet, when I think back, I don't know whether I liked to pray or not. My brother Leo and my youngest uncle, Andrew, disliked Babushka's insistence on regular prayer and often caused her trouble, but I did not misbehave during prayer time.

I especially loved my Babushka, for she was the only one who ever took time to mend my torn dresses or aprons before Mother got a look at them. She would have beaten the daylights out of me for climbing trees and tearing my clothes! I was quite a tomboy, so it often happened that Babushka covered up for me.

I've often thought about whether I loved the Lord back then, and I guess I'd have to say both yes and no. Today I know that Babushka planted the seed in my heart. She was

4

an example, not only to me but to the whole village.

Our church in the village was burned down but Babushka would take large shawls customarily worn by older Ukrainian women back then and hang them on the windows as shades. Then the people would come from everywhere to pray.

We no longer had priests. Many were chained to trucks and dragged to their deaths for refusing to "confess" that there is no God, or for refusing to deny their faith. Others were sent to Siberia, never to be seen again. At any rate, Babushka was the leader of the prayer meetings. She was not afraid of anyone. No man wanted the position and, as I recall, she had never volunteered—it just happened! They would often gather to pray, sing and praise the Lord. As a three-year-old child, and for several years thereafter, I saw large groups of people praying and kneeling on our living-room floor.

Of course, that kind of environment had a great effect on me. As a child growing up, it frightened me because the people wept a great deal. I can still see their faces, for they were deeply marked with the trouble and hardship that surrounded them. There was great suffering, not only in Mariaheim but in all the Ukraine. I always ran away from the crowds of people that gathered in our home, but I liked to have Babushka, Leo and Andrew, my brothers, pray with me.

These meetings continued for about eight years. However, by the time my two sisters, Luzia and Elisabeth, were born, prayer meetings were no longer allowed. The Communists became stricter and stricter and soon people stopped coming, one by one, until we were left alone to pray as a family.

One sister, Elvira, died as a baby. She was next to me; Luzia was almost five years younger and Elisabeth, whom we called Lisa, was eight years younger. How sad I was when my little sister died! My young heart suffered its first scar.

5

Chapter 2

FROM PLENTY TO POVERTY

My ancestors had originally migrated to Russia from Schwäbenland (Swabia), better known as Württemberg, Germany. They came at the time when Sophia Augusta Frederich, the German princess of Anhalt, became Catherine the Great of Russia on July 9, 1762. When she came to Russia she brought with her German settlers from Schleswig-Holstein, a state in Germany near Denmark's border, from Aachen, near Holland's border, and Württemberg, where my people came from. Catherine brought engineers, farmers and representatives of every major profession in order to help develop Russia. By the time World War II broke out, this settlement of Germans along the Volga River had multiplied to between six and nine million. It was a republic unto itself called Nemetchy Bovoltchy Republic, or the Volga German Republic.

We were farmers who lived and worked the land along the Dnieper River. The river's smooth, gleaming surface shone in the sunlight like silver armor as it made its way to the Black Sea. We were settled in one of the most beautiful sections of all of Russia, situated about eighty kilometers from Saporshia and eighty kilometers from Tchankoy, which is the gateway to Crimea, Russia's Florida. There one luxuriated at any of the Kurplaces (health spots) and tutchas (beaches) that abundantly dotted the area. We didn't live far from Odessa, Nikolayev, Dneprovskaya (once called Catherinaslav) and many other beautiful cities. My grandparents and parents were very happy there.

The land was rich chernozem soil, the blackest, richest soil in the world. In fact, the area was called the "Breadbasket

6

of Europe." Our houses, built out of white bricks, stood like proud birch trees. High, white brick walls stood sentinel in front of the houses. Beautiful abapala[1] trees framed both sides of the street. The United States does not have trees like them. Their leaves resemble oak leaves, but shine silvery on top with green undersides. When the slightest wind blew, the leaves would dance and tinkle like wind-chimes.

My father had been adopted by his uncle and aunt so I never knew my real grandparents. My father's parents were so-called "gentlemen farmers." They had maids and workers and every available piece of machinery with which to farm. They had cattle, sheep, horses, pigs, chickens, ducks—everything.

But tragedy struck and caused a fatal blow after the Revolution of 1917. Communism, the victor, took over when I was born in 1920 and totally controlled everything by 1928. They started to divide the land by taking it away from "gentlemen farmers." They gave it to the workers who had previously worked for them. This was the beginning of their original plan for equality in the Communist state.

At first everybody was given a certain amount of land, one cow, ten chickens and the house each lived in. But soon everything was taken from them also and, with it most of the men in the village. They were sent to Siberia as Kulaky[2] and were never heard from again. As far as the Communists were concerned, if one was branded a Kulaky, it was as if he had leprosy.

Fortunately, my father was spared in those years of 1926, 1927 and 1928 when a wave of arrests swept the villages and all the men were taken away. No spy could betray or sell him out to the N.K.W.D.[3] because Grandfather had failed to officially name my father an heir. They could not

---

[1] Abapala—a kind of poplar tree.
[2] Kulak—prosperous, wealthy peasant farmer of the 19th century in Russia.
[3] N.K.W.D., G.P.U., K.G.B.—abbreviated terms for secret police who are much feared by the populace.

touch him because they thought he was a worker and not a Kulaky.

Before long, the other workers approached my father, seeking help and advice which he really wasn't permitted to give. They were as helpless as little children with a new but complicated toy, they just didn't know how to work the land. They needed leadership and guidance, and they needed someone to tell them what to do. I remember how touching the situation was and how badly father felt for them.

My life was not easy. I was barely six years old when I had to help with the work. I don't seem to remember ever being a child, ever being young and carefree. It seems that I was old from the day I was born. One would never dream of asking your children to do the work I was asked to do by my father. I had to carry water as far as half a mile because our village only had two wells with sweet water. This I did with a half-full stomach. After the collective farms were started, I can't say there was a day when our stomachs did not grumble for more food. Most of the time our diet consisted of soup because there wasn't enough flour with which to bake bread. Oh, how precious a slice of bread was to us when we had it!

We didn't have many clothes to wear either. I had one pair of shoes and when the soles wore through, my father had to carry me to school or pull me on a sled. My mother washed our clothes after we went to bed, so we were kept warm while they dried by the fireplace.

By now I was in school and soon became a product of Communism. We received heavy indoctrination, much of which was absorbed by our young minds. At eight I had to join the October-Child Organization (thus called because of the October Revolution). At ten I became a Pioneer. At twelve I became a candidate for the Young-Comsomolist (like a Communist) but was refused because of my German heritage.

In spite of the rich Ukrainian soil, it seemed the crops were never sufficient. We were always hungry. The land was worked so poorly because most of the workers would say,

"Why should I bother to work hard when it isn't even mine?" But my father did not feel that way. He would say, "Oh, little children, we are all going to suffer for that because if the land is not worked well, there isn't going to be a harvest, and we'll all starve. Where do you think our bread will come from?" What he said was prophetic, for eventually what little rye and wheat grew on the neglected soil was insufficient to feed all the hungry people. There was a norm that collective farms had to maintain in order to feed the people of Russia. Communist troops would come to gather the tons of corn, rye and wheat and take it away, leaving very little behind. In 1932 there was a real famine in our area. The Governor of Ukraine, Gahanowitz, sent his troops to take everything we harvested. The Communists wanted to break the wills of the stubborn Ukrainian people because they silently resisted Communism.

At the time, my father was working on the pig farm for the "Kolchose" (nickname for collective farm). One day he was so hungry that he began to eat some of the beets and potato peelings he was feeding the pigs—it was really garbage. A party official from the "Kolchose" saw it and dismissed him immediately.

From then on my Dad's body began to swell for we had so little to eat. My two sisters and Mom were so thin—just bones and skin was left.

I was then twelve, and the only one of our family who was still able to work in the "Kolchose." I look back now and realize that God was with me, and that He was my strength. I worked seven days a week, from sunrise to sundown, and barely earned ten to twelve pounds of corn flour or grits. Mom would throw a few handfuls of meal into a pot of water to feed five people. In addition, we ate grass, tree bark and even dug the freshly planted seeds out of the soil. We no longer cared that nothing would grow.

Our people were so weak that the hot sun caused them to faint. They died on the sidewalks or in the streets, and nobody had the strength to bury their dead. Once a week a truck would come to pick up the dead and bury them in mass graves. My body was still the strongest of all the villagers. I would hoe rows of corn and sunflowers that were two miles long. Somewhere in the field stood a barrel with warm water, and since my lips were parched from the sun, I would walk to the barrel just to moisten them. But in spite of so little to eat, my stomach never pained me from the long fast.

Then one day an airplane flew over the villages and dropped leaflets. It was a Communist plane but the leaflets were written in German so I could read them. They said that if you were hungry, write to your neighbors in America, Germany and Austria. They had addresses of churches (remember, these were from unbelieving Communists). Since we had long ago broken off correspondence with relatives in Germany, I decided to write to the churches. In my childish, innocent way, I wrote telling them that I was twelve years old, had a father swollen from starvation, as well as two sisters and a mother who were also starving. (My brother Leo, who was eight years older than I, had disappeared and did not let us know of his whereabouts out of fear that the N.K.W.D. would take him.) The hope of a child is great, and so with that letter went my hope—the last hope for me and my family.

Chapter 3

THE DOUBLE GAME OF THE COMMUNISTS
SAVED OUR LIVES

Day after day we hung on to life, my family and I. We foraged for food in the woods, gathering mushrooms and flowers from the locust trees. We didn't care whether they were poisonous or not, but always God protected us. My father's swelling continued. He would have eaten us alive, his own children, if we had not confined him as one would an animal. (In fact, there were reports that the village three kilometers away did cook their children in large pots and eat them.) My sisters and mother were so thin and weak that they were barely able to walk. The whole land was very near death. There was no spring in anyone's walk—people dragged their feet as they walked. There was no smile on anybody's face. There was instead a deep, deep sadness.

But one day the sun broke through the clouds! I received a postcard from Melitopol, a town thirty kilometers away from us, telling me to report to the Torksin (government store) where money from Germany had arrived in my name. I could come and buy groceries and other necessities for the amount of ten marks. One stipulation was that I must bring an adult with me, so my mother elected herself to go with me to the Torksin.

We trudged the seven kilometers to the next railroad station at Fedarovka, and rode the rest of the distance by train. The ride seemed like an eternity, for my thoughts were with my father and sisters who were in such desperate need. I feared I was dreaming and would wake up to find death standing at our door, instead of life just a few kilometers away.

When we finally arrived at the store, our eyes almost popped out at seeing the abundance displayed there. Our hearts beat faster just to look at the beautiful french bread, lemons, tea, sugar, raisins and so much more than what we had seen for a long time. I felt like Gretel standing in front of the gingerbread house in the middle of the forest. Here was plenty in the midst of starvation.

For ten marks we got as much as $50 would buy today. My mother and I were loaded down with bundles. But after we left Fedorovka, I expressed fear to my mother at seeing the people sitting and lying along both sides of the road. She reprimanded me, saying that these were the least to fear for how would starving, half-dead people harm us? We got through safely, but I shall never forget the sight of those starving people who cried out to us for a morsel to eat. We were forced to ignore them, knowing that my own father and sisters waited at home for this life-giving food.

One would think we had a feast that night, but we didn't for we knew it could have killed us if we filled our stomachs after they had been empty for so long. Dad especially screamed for more food but we denied him, knowing we had to eat more gradually. I received two more postcards before the 1933 harvest which sustained us and kept us alive.

Have you wondered why the Communists were so kind to us, so "out of character" for their usual pattern of behavior? There were reasons the Torksins were set up and we were urged to write to other countries. In 1932 the Communists had come to the conclusion that their regime was faltering and their country bankrupt, so they devised a clever scheme to save themselves and Communism.

Their machinery—combines, plows, tractors, etc.—had been imported mostly from Germany, but some also came from America. They needed parts to fix these machines but had to have foreign money with which to buy parts. They had no money, so they set up stores in large cities with everything available to customers. But in these stores you could only buy with foreign currency, dollars, marks or sterling.

Then they dropped leaflets over the villages, urging the starving people to write to relatives and churches in foreign countries, telling of their plight and needs.

When I first brought the leaflets home, my father saw through the scheme. He said it was a trick of the devil. He pointed out that anyone of age writing a letter would eventually be sent to Siberia as *"free labor."*[1] He refused to write a letter because he felt the Communists were only "killing two birds with one stone"—money to get parts and free labor. He proved to be right, but I was only twelve so they did not touch me.

Finally the harvest of 1933 was ready to reap, but by then the people of the villages were so weak that nearly the whole harvest would have remained wherever it grew had not the city people come to help us.

After the harvest it was a little easier. Starvation had been kept at bay through the generosity of the Germans, British, Americans, Austrians and other friends of the Russian peasants.

Now Dad, strengthened once again, would disappear at night and come home a little later with a huge bag of flour. He had befriended a man who was in charge of the Communist windmill. Here flour was ground for the collective farmers in the communes. He would scrape up and steal as much as 32 lbs. of flour at a time, and then he would sell it to my father for a considerable sum of money. My father brought it home and my mother would bake bread with it.

The next day I'd rise early and walk a long distance to school, stopping at the railroad station to await the arrival of the train. There I stood with the bread my mother had baked secretly the night before, and I would sell it by the slice to the hungry passengers. After I had taken in the amount of money my father needed to buy more flour, I'd go to school. After a hard, long day at school my joy was to bring the money from the bread sold at the station and some left over slices for my family to eat. This is how we got along for many years.

---

[1] A prisoner of a slave camp.

Chapter 4

MY HIDDEN BITTERNESS AND CONDEMNATION
AGAINST MY MOTHER

My mother had a very hard life. She lived in the Crimea before she married my Dad. Her parents had a large family; she had nine brothers and three sisters. All her brothers died tragic deaths. The last one to die was Andrew, her most beloved brother. He was sent to Siberia in 1933 because he had married an American girl. Her name was Caroline Pope. She came from a wealthy Midwestern family. She had met my Uncle Andrew while visiting Russia. The "crime" my uncle committed was that he continued to correspond with her family in America.

One day I saw my mother holding a letter and crying. It told of her brother Andrew's death in Siberia. A friend of his wrote to her (in those days, political prisoners could still write home) and told how they slept on filthy straw that was never changed. It was full of lice and bugs. Uncle got so weak that he wasn't able to go to work in the forest any longer. The Communists stopped feeding him saying, "Whoever doesn't work doesn't eat." So he became weaker and weaker. The parasites ate right through his heart. One day he went to the latrine and didn't return. His friend found him dead.

No wonder my mother was crushed. No wonder she was always crying and always angry with us. I did not understand then for I was never comfortable around her. I'd rather run to Grandma for she was always happy, never down. Who wants to be around sad and negative people? Besides, I think I subconsciously rebelled against my mother.

There was a time, shortly before Dad and I were sent to labor camp, when Mom was especially hard on Dad. She was

14

always complaining that he never did anything right. She nagged him continually for not taking proper care of his family. Dad always took this verbal abuse silently and never attempted to defend himself.

He would always try, but in her eyes he failed. This particular time he had taken butter and eggs from the villagers in order to sell them at the bazaar (market place). It was very hot in the summer and by the time he got there the butter was rancid, so he only received half its normal worth. Attempting to make up for the loss he bought fish, hoping it would please the women at home. But, again, the heat spoiled the fish and it smelled terrible by the time he got home. The people of the village loved Dad and told him it did not matter, but he felt the burden of responsibility and paid them back as best he could. This time Mother would not let up on him but pouted and nagged and complained so much that for once Dad had his fill. He didn't say a word but took his hat and cane and silently left the house.

Somehow, though I was only thirteen, I sensed the seriousness of this act. An icy hand of fear gripped my heart for I knew something frightful would happen. I slipped out of the house, trailing after him through the garden and into the forest. My feet could hardly keep up with his pace, but he heard me approaching and waited for me. When I got to him I grasped his hand with both of mine and asked, "Where are you going, Dad?"

He looked at me so pitifully and so in despair, that I can still see his face before my eyes. He said, "I will go as far as my legs will carry me. Your mother is right. I am nothing but trouble. Everything I do fails. I'm no good to any of you. I am a jinx and you are better off without me."

There it was. He had said it. It was what I feared most. My little lips quivered and I cried pleadingly, "Please don't go, Dad. Don't go. I love you, Dad. Don't leave us." I pleaded and pleaded with him, my heart almost breaking.

Finally he said, "I always thought you were made of stone because you never cried. Even when your mother beat

15

you, you still did not cry. And now, tears?"

I won! With a leap in my heart I kissed his hand and we returned home. From that day on something in me resented my mother. As young as I was, I was against her. I couldn't understand why she didn't see how desperately Dad tried. Even when he cut trees down at night from our own place, he was breaking the law in order to warm our home. The Communists' intent was to strip the men of Russia of their manhood, their self-sufficiency. Dad's hands were tied. He wanted so to be the head of his household. One could read the agony in his quiet, brown eyes.

My Dad treated everyone with kindness. When all the men in the village had been whisked away, he helped their families, knowing full well he, too, was marked. His suitcase was always ready, for he knew that when the N.K.W.D. came they wouldn't wait for him to pack.

But while he was home, he helped all the women and children in the village. There were roofs to be mended, brick stoves to be rebuilt, or what have you. He went everywhere helping everybody. He didn't belong exclusively to our family any longer. He belonged to everyone, and yet he never complained.

Chapter 5

THE DREAM THAT KEPT ME GOING

When I was fourteen years old, the Communists came and signed up my father and me to work on construction at a labor camp in Nishna-Petrovsk (Upper-Petrovsk) and Verchna-Petrovsk (Lower-Petrovsk) where a huge meat factory was being built. We were always hungry at the collective farms so were trying to better our lot, but we didn't know what we were letting ourselves in for. The work we did was most difficult. We young girls pushed huge wheelbarrows filled with stones, sand, gravel and bricks. All day long my Dad had to work in frigid areas where meat was frozen. He had frost bite on both ears so bad that they turned black. We cooked our meager meals between two bricks and it was such bad food that we gladly volunteered to peel potatoes at night so we could steal some for ourselves.

We slept in one big room in the barracks. The beds were so infested with lice and bedbugs that the moment the lights went out they began to suck our poor blood. In the morning our eyes were swollen and our whole bodies were covered with bites.

We were beaten when some of us talked among ourselves in German, or when we did not produce the norm we were given to do. We lost half the workers under the piles of gravel and stone. A lot of them just didn't have the will to live any more and just gave up.

I don't know what made me go on, but I believe it was the hope that still burned within me—that I would go to America some day. In the midst of dirt and starvation, with rags on my body and rag wrap-arounds on my feet, I would imagine myself in the giant stores of America surrounded by

17

all the ice cream I could eat, as well as cakes, cookies, oranges and white bread. Often I would see myself in a beautiful white dress flowing down to my knees, a white hat with a wide brim to protect my eyes from the sun and, of course, I'd have on long, white gloves that went up to my elbows. To top it off, on my feet I'd be wearing beautiful, sparkling white shoes. Then I'd see myself slipping into the most elegant car you ever did see (we didn't even have bicycles). Yet I pictured that vision, and it kept me going.

I did not have a Bible with me for Bibles were forbidden, but I knew I was not alone. I knew God in heaven watched over me. When I closed my eyes I could see in my mind's eye the greatest Eye in all the world beholding us. I didn't pray, for I did not know how, but I had a peace beyond understanding. Yes, I even sang Russian Ukrainian songs and danced in the dusty streets whenever an accordian or harmonica played. I can honestly say I did not cry, complain or grumble but took everything as it came, always expecting good things. When they didn't happen that day, I'd look to the next, keeping in my mind my vision of America. I'm glad I didn't realize then how long twenty-six years are to wait.

Chapter 6

LOVE AT FIRST SIGHT

In the spring we finally went home. Shortly after our return a group of men showed up at our collective farm (named, ironically, "Ahead" though we never seemed to get ahead at all). They came to mobilize girls from sixteen to eighteen for a course at the Machine Tractor Station (MTS) that would train them how to operate and repair tractors. I volunteered for six months as I wanted to get away from the village. I told them I was older so that I could be accepted.

At MTS we had classes every day in theory, driving and repairing machines. Those six months were the best of my life in Ukraine for we had plenty of borsch, bread and kasha.[1] No, I was not hungry anymore. I worked hard, studied hard and did not starve. When the six months were over, I was asked to stay four more months for a course in combine operating, as they were just becoming popular on collective farms.

One day an order came from headquarters to move the school from Fredricksfield to Hochstadt. At first I was disappointed because I was so content there with plenty of food, a good bed in which to sleep and overalls to wear. I had met wonderful companions and had good teachers. I wanted to stay, but I dismissed my disappointment and looked forward to the move.

Shortly after my arrival at MTS I had met Nicky, a good-looking Ukrainian engineer. He was twelve years older than I, but it was love at first sight. Besides having blue eyes and

---

[1] Millet—a popular national cereal cooked in water or milk until thick like porridge.

19

dark brown, wavy hair, he was a good musician. He played the accordian, violin, guitar and balalaika. It seemed he could play every instrument he picked up. I felt young, alive and happy. I thought my luck had changed.

He took me to meet his family. His father, mother and brother looked like aristocrats because they were such handsome people, especially his father. He had soft brown eyes, grey hair and a well-groomed mustache. His mother looked more German than I with her long, blonde hair flowing to her hips, her blue eyes and elegant figure. They seemed to like me, and we got along well.

Next we went to visit my folks. My long-lost brother Leo was home visiting my parents while I was away. He had married a Ukrainian girl, Tanja Maslenkova. So while my future husband Nicky talked with my parents, my brother and sister-in-law took me aside in the next room. My brother, who stood 6'4" tall, took off his belt and started to beat me for wanting to get married so young. My father came to my rescue and rebuked my brother with the remark that Leo could beat his own children some day if he had any, but he was not to beat his sister. The rest of the evening passed peacefully.

Chapter 7

MY MARRIAGE BROUGHT JOY AND SUFFERING

On May 2, 1936 we were married. I was young, just sixteen, but I knew suffering, I knew responsibility and I knew commitment. I was tired of all of them. For once in my life I wanted to have someone to care for me instead of me always being the oldest and taking care of everybody else. I wanted someone to lean on. Nicky was not a big man in stature, but he was loving and he always brought his pay home. We didn't have a luxurious apartment for it only had one room and a kitchen, but we were happy.

On our wedding night I became pregnant, and our first child Lucy was born February 2, 1937. She was a beautiful child and looked just like her father. He was so proud of her that he didn't want to put her down. But something was wrong with her for she cried incessantly. I was young and ignorant and didn't understand why her little fists were clenched and her nails dug into the palms of her hands. So I called an older woman from the building who took one look at her and knew what was wrong. My baby was dying. Being a believer, she took water and baptized her in the name of the Father and of the Son and of the Holy Spirit. That night our daughter died in her father's arms, quietly falling asleep. She rests in South Ukraine at Hochstadt Cemetery. She lived only twelve days.

Soon after Lucy's death, my in-laws suggested that we move to the city of Molotchansk and build a house together. I had learned that my husband and in-laws were Communists—full-fledged members of the Communist party, but it made no difference to me one way or the other; it was too late.

It didn't take long to find out what a mistake we had made. I hardly ever saw my husband alone again after we began to live with his parents. At first he would ask his mother if I could go out with him, but she always had things for me to do and soon Nicky didn't ask anymore. I became a slave to his family. My husband, his brother and I worked, and we had to bring our pay envelope home, unopened, to my father-in-law. I never had a kopaka (cent) for my own use. They insisted that I was too young to know the value of money, and they were determined to continue treating me like a little child.

After Nicky would leave, his mother would make me wash her feet and then strip her bed and wash her bed linen by hand. There was a dirt floor in the house and because the soil was so rich, fleas were always a problem.

Washing our laundry was no easy matter. We had no running water and the well we had gave only hard, bitter water. Again I had to walk for water—to the heart of the city. But this time it was one-and-a-half miles that I had to carry two buckets of water on a goromisla (yoke over the neck) to wash clothes, cook and drink. That took many trips. When we had rain we gathered the rain water instead for washing the clothes.

This way of life went on and on, and for the first time in my life, my sorrow went to the depths of my soul. We had a chicken coop where I would go at night and cry my heart out. It was the first time in my life that I cried. I'd look towards heaven through my tears for answers, but I never really expected any at all. For the first time my dreams for America seemed hopeless. I was trapped. I was imprisoned in my own home. I had a husband and yet I was a slave of slaves. I dared not say anything to Nicky because I was now afraid of him. He had changed and didn't seem to care for me any longer. My parents were not allowed to visit me. I could go to them but when I complained to them about my trials my mother would say, "You made your bed, now sleep in it. You can't come home. Think of what the people in the village would say. The shame of it. No, no, I won't stand for that!"

The situation got worse and worse. One day my father-in-law made an especially big commotion. He called my husband and his brother into one of the rooms, opened a closet where money was thrown around on the floor. He claimed that he had caught me stealing and thirty rubles were missing. He acted it out so convincingly that they believed what he said. My father-in-law insisted that Nicky should divorce me, but I was pregnant again so he refused.

I continued to work in a military factory, faithfully bringing my pay to my father-in-law, always unopened for fear of a beating. I could never prove my innocence regarding the accusation that I had stolen thirty rubles. Only God and I knew that I had never touched any money.

Chapter 8

TWENTIETH CENTURY JUDAS

In 1939, close to the birth of my child, I approached my father-in-law with a trembling heart to request money for the baby's clothing. He refused, saying that my mother-in-law would handle that. The subject was closed.

On June 28th I went to my mother's. She was now alone with my sisters for my father had been taken by the N.K.W.D. at midnight on October 18, 1937, on his fiftieth birthday. He had been betrayed by the village spy for having a prayer book with scripture readings in his possession. He was shipped to Siberia on the heels of so many other men of Russia.

My Dad was a quiet man who never swore nor cursed anyone. He loved the soil he walked on, for it was "God's earth," as he would often say. He loved trees and was always planting them, often grafting one to another, experimenting. We had rosebushes with four different varieties and colors. Yellow, white, pink, red and orange were among some of the beautiful shades of his roses. We had rows and rows of apricots, as well as every other kind of fruit tree.

Before the collective farms were formed and took everything away, he had a private little forest in the back of the orchard that was the park of the village. In it were selected trees from all over the world. To Dad's disappointment, however, he could not grow pine trees. Our soil was free of rocks and far too rich to grow them. I wish with all my heart he could see the pine trees we have in America.

Dad was an innocent, hard-working man, who did not deserve the punishment he received at the hands of the Communists. Each village had its spies and so did Mariaheim. His

24

name was Joe Krebs. He happened to be the herdsman for our village who brought the cows out to the pastures to graze. Father had always been kind to Joe and treated him better than any other man he knew. My father respected all men and women, knowing them to be God's creation just as he knew the earth and trees to be God's creation. Perhaps this prevented Joe from betraying him sooner, but times were hard and money was scarce. The Communists pressed him until, finally, Joe turned him in for 300 rubles. (Joe had also betrayed my Aunt Julia's husband, and then had the nerve to move into her house, leaving one room for her and her three children.)

I've often wondered how he felt, receiving all that blood money. It was no small matter that my father wrote from prison, asking for us all to pray for that man. Father said he would rather be where he was than to be in Joe Krebs' shoes. He knew his betrayer because he had faced him before the Troyka (three accusers) and yet he still forgave him. He constantly asked for us to pray and forgive him, too.

When a letter would come to my mother, all the women of the village would come to find out if Dad had seen their husbands, sons or brothers. Unfortunately, no one he knew was with him. Only two other Russian-born Germans like himself were there, but they came from the Crimea. The rest of the men were Ukrainians and Russians.

We were lucky to receive occasional letters from Father. Most families from the surrounding villages never heard from their men once they were sent to Siberia. Their secrets are buried in the Siberian forests. Only God knows how many seeds of good Ukrainian blood have been planted. Some day those seeds will sprout forth tenfold against the Communists. Then they will grow like a gigantic, invisible, uncontrollable force, demanding revenge and restitution to mankind.

When I saw him on my last visit before the Communists took him, we had a good talk. I remember saying I didn't think they'd come for him because he was innocent. He got angry with me, asking if I truly believed all the rest of the

25

men they had taken were guilty. And I, brain-washed as I was from school indoctrination and the thinking of my Communist husband, said, "Dad, they must be. Why would the police pick them up if they weren't?" Before I could say another word, he struck me on the mouth. I never saw him again. Can you imagine how I felt?

Mom told me later how he had placed his hands on my sisters' heads and blessed them before leaving the house. He sent a greeting to Ella, as he always called me, and a message that he didn't fear for me. He said I'd get through the world unbroken, but he feared for my little sisters for they were timid.

My father was sentenced to twenty-five years. They tortured him by putting him in a cellar partially filled with ice-cold water. They tried to force him to deny God but he refused saying, "Let me freeze to death, I will not deny God." He was sent to Amur, where it is six months day and six months night.

When he had served three years of his sentence the authorities said there was nothing wrong with him and he was sent back to Kharkov to have his case reviewed. But his enemies were still in power and this time they sentenced him to Archangel on the Ice Sea. He wrote one letter from there in July and said the icicles were then the size of a man's arm. He wrote to them, "You will never see me again on earth. Think of me as dead and as not among the living."

I helped my mother clean and cook during my visit because she had lost her right hand due to blood poisoning from getting a splinter in her finger at the collective farm.

Early on the morning of June 30th I went into premature labor. There was no time to go back to my in-laws' home and, as I expected, I had nothing for my baby to wear. When the mid-wife notified my mother-in-law, she cut up old sheets and made the first clothes for my son Arnold. (He is now thirty-eight years old and lives in America).

The real trouble began when I went back with my baby.

He was not allowed to cry. In their old age, they would not stand for a crying baby in their house. Well, neither would I stand for their complaints any longer. I packed my suitcase, took my baby and left, never to return.

I remember walking from house to house with my son, searching for a room to stay. Finally a widow took us in. We had nothing; no furniture, just the few possessions I had packed in one suitcase. Yet, life went on. I worked and brought my child to the child care center (Yasly) near the factory. Nothing mattered now except my baby.

One day I came out of work and found my husband Nick standing there with his suitcase. He asked, "Where do we live?" I wondered at the time how he got the nerve to leave his parents at thirty-one years of age, but I only said, "Follow me."

Things were somewhat better after that. At least I was not enslaved to my in-laws any longer. But it did not last long; Nick really didn't want to accept the responsibility of a wife and son.

Chapter 9

THE FLOOD AND THE TWO MYSTERIOUS RIDERS

One day I left the baby with our landlady Sophia, who was a very good woman. I went by train to see my mother and sisters again as I visited them now as often as possible. It was spring and the snow was melting. It was slushy but not muddy as in other parts of Russia.

But no sooner did I get to my mother's and say hello when I immediately felt urged to go back home. When I told my mother she gasped, "Impossible! Don't you know what this weather means?"

"No," I said, "I don't, and I don't want to know, either. I only know I must go back at once." I calculated how much time I had until the train left and came to the conclusion that I'd make it. So I said good-bye and out I went.

I had to walk seven kilometers from my mother's village, and there were no homes on the way. You must understand that Russia is not thickly settled as is America or other well-populated countries. South Ukraine was all flat farm land with no mountains or forests. I suppose it could be compared to our Midwest.

So, as I left town and had walked about 1 kilometer, it seemed out of nowhere water began to slowly rise up all around me. My first thought was to go back to the village, but it was too late. The sunny day had rapidly melted all the snow and it was flooding the flat land. I had valenky (felt boots) on my feet and soon the water rose over them and continued to rise. My coat was soon soaked and I began to get panicky because I could not swim.

The situation quickly got worse. Then it wasn't only the rising water I had to worry about, but great pieces of ice began to come rushing toward me. They brushed against me nearly knocking me down, but I struggled to keep my footing. The water was now nearly up to my chin and I realized I was going to drown. With my last bit of strength I looked up to heaven and yelled, "Help!"

Instantly two riders came out of nowhere (or so it seemed) and rode up to me, ordering me to climb up on the horse behind one of them. They asked me where I was going, and I told them my destination. They brought me to the railroad station, never uttering a word all the way. They dropped me off, rode away, disappearing from sight, and I never saw them again.

I bought my ticket with soaking wet money. I was wet clear through. Wherever I stood I left behind a puddle of water. I caught the train just in time and returned home to Molotchansk. There Sophia and Nicky had to cut the boots off my feet and the clothes off my back. I soaked my feet in hot water, drank a glass of vodka and went to bed. I went to work the very next day and never had a cold or any after-effects whatsoever.

Chapter 10

IMPRISONMENT FOR BEING BRANDED
A BLACK MARKETEER

We still lacked many necessities such as soap, sugar and thread to mend our clothing. My mother and sisters were suffering very much.

One day on my trip to our village of Mariaheim, I met people on the train who told me that the miners at the Stalino coal mines got everything they needed. They were treated better because coal was very important to the Russian industry. They received a book with stamps to fulfill all their needs. They had special privileges and could shop at special stores. These people on the train gave me addresses of where to go, people to see and even places where I could stay.

On my arrival at my mother's, I immediately shared this news, not only with Mom but with other relatives from the village. We came to a decision. They would all give me a list of what they needed and give me money and would split the expenses for my trip. My sisters would care for my baby.

Off I went by train from Fedorovka to the Stalino coal mines. It proved to be exactly as I had been told. I made immediate contact with certain miners whose names had been given to me, bought stamps from them and then went shopping in their stores.

These trips were frequent. I would bring back sweaters, dresses, yard goods, thread, soap, sugar and many other things we were unable to obtain in the south of the Ukraine. But alas, jealousy found its way into the heart of a man who had once gone to school with me. He was the husband of my best girlfriend from childhood years. He reported me to the secret police, who arrested me when I stepped off the train on one of my return trips. They confiscated everything.

People I knew had been arrested for no obvious reason other than perhaps complaining while standing in line for hours for bread or some other similar minor infraction of the Communist rules. They would then be taken to prison and many never returned. Sometimes it seemed spies were everywhere and it even appeared that Communists must have read our very thoughts, so quickly were people arrested. But now, here they were picking me up.

My first thought was for my child. I thought that perhaps no one would even know what had happened to me and I'd simply disappear forever. I'd never see my son nor my husband nor family again.

I was brought to Michilovka prison and charged with conducting a black market. They accused me of buying items for a low price and reselling them for double and triple the cost.

I was alone in the cold cell with all the tragic writing on the walls and the ghosts of the people who had previously been confined in this very cell. I had no food nor blankets to warm me. I wore the same clothes day after day. I paced the floor. I sat. I could not sleep so I did the only thing I was free to do. I thought.

I thought about the miners in Stalino who really had nothing to spare but needed the money to buy vodka to dull their pain. They all looked so pale and thin. I remembered how they had all looked so sick in body and soul.

I thought about God. I didn't know too much about Him, except that He was way off in heaven somewhere. The Communists always told us that if there was a God, He would be banished by them to Siberia. I didn't know of His love for me nor even how to call on Him, but I didn't see God in Siberia for in my mind He was too big to be confined anywhere on earth. But though I didn't know God, He still knew me and was working out this latest problem in my life. He, after all, is the best lawyer ever, and God never slumbers nor sleeps, but works for us twenty-four hours a day.

31

Somehow my husband found out where I was. To my advantage he was a party member and was not afraid to approach the president of the Communist party in Molotchansk where we lived. He explained the situation and was told to get a petition signed by all the people for whom I had bought goods in Stalino. They witnessed that I had not overcharged them but only received what each item had cost in Stalino. At midnight, September 23, 1939, all charges against me were dismissed and I was released.

Chapter 11

THE JOY OF OUR REUNION

I never got the suitcases back that had been confiscated, but I didn't care because I was so glad to be free. When they first led me out of my cell and told me I was to be set free, I thought, "Oh, yeah? First you let me out and then as I walk away, you'll shoot me in the back." This often happened to others. But I didn't speak my thoughts. Instead I lifted my shoulders to ward off the fear gripping me and walked briskly away into the dark. I really was free!

I walked, ran and stumbled the eighteen kilometers to my mother's house. The night was pitch black for there was no moon to light the dirt road. There wasn't one house all the way to Mariaheim, and as I approached each wooded area I held my breath for fear that bandits would be lurking there. They say it is darkest before the dawn and so it proved that night, for as daylight broke upon the land, the shadows softened and my fear melted away.

I soon saw the village in the distance and ran the rest of the way, the joy welling up in my being. I found my mother's house, looked in the window and beheld my mother going about the business of preparing for a new day. She turned and saw me standing there and let out a cry. She told me later that she thought I was a ghost—that they had killed me and I had returned as a specter. No one came back once they were imprisoned, so it was indeed a natural reaction.

But I yelled and pounded at the door until she finally opened the door and let me in. I think I saw my mother smiling at me for the first time in my life for she was truly happy to see me.

What a reunion we had in Mariaheim! The whole village

got together, and Babushka praised the Lord like never before! She had been praying for my return. You cannot beat a faithful Babushka. The Communists feared them, for even though they had no sword nor might, they had spirit. They were not afraid to die. Babushka would say, "Let them send me to Siberia. I'll never get there for I'm too old and they cannot kill me twice."

She had one daughter Julia, three sons, one son-in-law and my father, who was her stepson. All five men were taken out of her life and sent to Siberia. She loved them all, never making any preferences. She comforted her daughter-in-law, her daughter and my mother. They could not have gotten along without her support. She also had fourteen grandchildren, and she loved us all. Though my Dad was her stepson, I was still her favorite grandchild. I think it was because I always listened to her when she talked about God, whereas the others got bored and left. I loved her so much that I could not displease her in anything.

No matter how happy we were to be reunited that day, the stark reality of our miserable life had not departed. We had a saying among ourselves, "We live on love and air." When mealtime came Mother had the toughest job of all. What could she cook? What would she serve us? Our household was somewhat better off than many others, however. Out of loyalty and love for my father, our Ukrainian friends would bring crude flax linen for her to make shirts and blouses. Mother crocheted, knitted and embroidered beautifully, so she would spend nights making clothes for our neighbors. In return, they'd pay her with groceries: flour, grits, potatoes, butter and sometimes even a side of smoked ham.

My Dad also had some good Jewish friends who were dealers when he was a gentleman farmer. They, too, gave her work so that she would not feel like a charity case. They all knew of her great pride; she would rather have died than take things for nothing.

34

Chapter 12

MIRACLES IN RUSSIA UNDER THE COMMUNISTS' NOSES

After I was released from prison in Michilovka and picked up my son at my mother's, I went back to my husband as soon as possible. I was grateful to him for pulling strings and getting me released.

Soon after getting home, my baby took sick and had to be hospitalized. Days went by, but he didn't get better. If anything, he got worse. After having lost Lucy, I was very worried that Arnold would also die. He looked blue and his little hands were cramped tight shut. I was told he had mlatjeuchiski, a common ailment babies have in Russia. They have cramps so badly that their entire body gets twisted.

As I stood over his crib looking at him one day when he was so very ill, I turned around to find a young man standing in the doorway. He came over and looked down at the sick baby and said, "Get your baby dressed and get out of here as quickly as possible. Here's an address. My mother lives there and she'll know what to do."

He seemed so assured that she could help my baby that I took a chance. Something had to be done or Arnold would surely die. I decided to follow his directions. I dressed the baby, wrapped him in a blanket, pressed him to my chest and went out. I almost ran the three kilometers to the outskirts of the city where the young man's mother lived. The thought remained that I was taking a big chance, but I felt compelled to seek help. I just couldn't stand by and watch my child die.

When I got to the address, the woman whom I was seeking answered the door. She let me in and I told her that her son had said she could help my baby. She seemed to know

35

exactly what she was doing. She took Arnold in her arms, un-wrapped him and, sitting with him in her lap, she put one hand on his forehead and another under his little head. She began to pray over him in a way which really seemed different to me at the time.

After several minutes she turned to me and said, "You look like you need rest. Come, lie down. I'll take care of your child." And for the first time in days I slept for hours—a deep, restful sleep. Later I learned that the baby had slept just as soundly and peacefully as I.

When we awakened, she strengthened us with food and quietly sent us on our way. She asked me not to tell anyone what had happened and, of course, I never did. From that day on, my child was well. He didn't cry anymore and grew rapidly. To my surprise he walked and talked within eight months' time and got his teeth all at once, it seemed. He never had trouble teething and was a happy little fellow.

Though I witnessed my first miracle, I still did not know God. He seemed far away and not inside my heart. I gave little thought to sin, and my heart belonged very much to the world. I wanted nice clothing, beautiful furniture and a home of my own. I was perfectly content to have God remain somewhere at a distance while I went on doing my own thing. Now I am grateful that God was with me even then. He's always a faithful God whose eyes go to and fro over all the world watching over His riches and glory, His creation. It seems to me as I reflect back, that God turned every curse I encountered into a blessing. The Lord turned around every bit of evil. He rescued me and then poured blessings on top of it all. How thick the veil was over my eyes that I could see and not understand! I knew there was a God but could not grasp Him. I knew little about Him. I didn't know that He gave His only begotten Son for me that I might live. I didn't know Jesus purchased me with His own blood, that He bought me and freed me from sin and slavery. No, I knew nothing of this. I saw miracles but coldly shrugged my shoulders saying, "So what? He's a big God. The whole world can't contain Him." But I failed to understand that He could be small enough to come into my heart. That I had never heard. Not even Babushka told me about that. I wonder now how much my Babushka kept secret in her heart. She sure loved the Lord. As little as she was, she worked like a giant, never tiring of doing things for people no matter who they were, and there was always a peace about her; I never remember hearing her complain.

Chapter 13

BEGINNING OF WORLD WAR II

The next two years were uneventful for we lived from day to day; nothing worse or better than usual. Every night I'd go and stand in line for bread so that when the bakery opened I'd be near the front of the line, for usually there was no bread left for those who were at the end of the line. Besides, I had to go to work on time. We stood there when it was cold, in the middle of a blizzard, or in sweltering heat. We dared not complain because it could worsen our situation. Spies were all around, even in bread lines. Neighbors often disappeared because they dared to grumble about the tiring nightly wait in line, and then having to go to work in the morning. How dare they murmur about this paradise that the Communists had created for us in Russia! After all, no other country had it so good they would tell us. And the Communists who escaped from Hitler's regime supported this lie. There was propaganda all around us from morning until evening, telling us how bad the West was.

Molotchansk was a clean city and all the homes were built during the Czarist period so that the style was typical of that time, with its spires and domes. We had a lot of industry in the city, especially military factories. We had some breweries, too. There were a lot of stores, but all of them were empty. I never knew the population of the city but I would estimate it to be 30,000 to 40,000.

Sometimes I was overwhelmed by the thought that we'd spend our entire life in this way. It was monotonous and so routine. If you missed the bazaar at a certain time, you wouldn't have beets, carrots, potatoes, cabbage or other vegetables until next time, and one could not make borsch. If a

38

Ukrainian doesn't have borsch,[1] bread and kasha, he's really hungry! And so it seemed we were always waiting for better times, but instead it always got worse—inferior products, higher prices and greater norms. Norms in factories were always being raised but our pay stayed the same.

On June 22, 1941 radios blasted throughout the city that Russia was at war with Germany. I distinctly remember my landlady Sophia crying and I could not understand this. I was happy. Yes indeed, I was happy. Finally things would change—either for better or for the worse but, thank God, it would no longer be the way it was. The stale air would change, it would circulate again. There would be ups and downs but at least things would not be at a standstill.

And so it was. In no time at all there was so much excitement that we never knew what hit us. First, my husband was immediately drafted. I was five months pregnant and had a two-year-old, but I was not worried. At least I wasn't worried yet, for I honestly thought the war would soon be over. I couldn't even imagine that it wouldn't end until every drop of blood was squeezed from us. At night we'd go into bomb shelters and during the day at work we were constantly interrupted by sirens—up, down, up again, down again into the underground shelters (which were no more than dirt holes). It is a good thing I didn't know what was ahead!

There were rumors everywhere—none of them good, a lot were guessing, some was conjecture, some was truth, especially about our Jewish friends. Many of them heard what Hitler would do to them and left before the Germans came.

I thought much about this and what a hateful, evil world this was. We had three nationalities in our family. My youngest uncle Andrew was Jewish. My brother Leo and I were married to Ukrainians. We, though born in Russia, were always marked by the Communists as German "pigs." We wanted to forget our heritage, but they would not let us.

---

[1] Borsch or borscht a soup made primarily of beets and served hot or cold with sour cream.

Now each one in our family was afraid for the other's welfare. The older people were especially depressed and frightened. My poor Babushka had been married to a Jewish man before she married Grandpa and was torn down the middle. She didn't like the Communists, but with terror in her eyes she received the news of what Hitler was doing. She knew we were going to be scattered in different directions for different reasons and by different enemies. But our love for one another knew no boundary nor nationality. Even though we were a family of various nationalities, we faced the enemy squarely in the face, staring him in the eye, and no matter what his name, we knew that whether his name was Communism or Nazism, one was as bad as the other and none had the interest of the people at heart for they were all driven by the same Satanic power.

I still visited my husband who was twenty kilometers away from home in the suburbs of Militopol. There recruits were on standby waiting for the southern Ukrainian army to be called to battle. The last time I went with my son to visit his father was somehow different from the other times. There was a restlessness among the soldiers and officers. Here I was pregnant and already had one child to care for. I somehow sensed that my husband would be shipped out to the front line, and I was quite disturbed by all of this. On top of it, they heard me talking; and having been raised with my mother's language, I spoke Russian with a German accent. I didn't think anything of it or realize I was different. Because my husband was Ukrainian I felt that my marriage to him made me Ukrainian also.

They questioned Nicky about his wife being German. This alarmed him so he urged us to leave as quickly as possible for he feared for our lives. I took my son and left. We walked about six kilometers and stayed overnight in a bomb shelter at a nearby village. After that I was cautious and only spoke when absolutely necessary.

That was the last time I saw Nicky for he was shipped to the front line to fight the Germans soon after. Most of them defected to the Germans because they realized that they had no cause for which to fight and die. I never found out what happened to my husband. I don't know whether he lived or was killed. No matter how I tried to find out, it was in vain. I was declared a widow at twenty-one. I was tired. Again I was alone with a child to support and another on its way. I had no one to help me but God. He alone continued to be faithful; and, though I didn't recognize it at the time, He moved me around as though I was on a chessboard.

Chapter 14

THE GERMAN ARMY TAKES OVER

When I came back to the city of Molotchansk, there was a great uproar about every German born in Russia. The Communists would go from house to house picking them up. As yet I was spared because I had a Ukrainian name. At the railroad station of Boluhorod (half-city), there were thousands of Russian-born Germans waiting to be shipped out. They just lay there or sat there waiting.

No one knew, of course, that the station director's wife was also of German descent. He kept it quiet, but he worked for them nevertheless. As thousands of people waited under guard to be sent to Siberia, he manipulated army trains and freight cars, telling the Communist authorities that they were needed for more urgent tasks like sending ammunition and supplies and were not available for use in shipping people to Siberia. He laid his life on the line to save and protect the people.

I didn't stay long in the city for it was being bombed continually and, being with child and carrying a heavy two-year-old, I found it increasingly difficult to get around. So I decided to go to my mother's house once more. I figured it would at least be quiet there since the Germans only bombed the cities where there was heavy industry.

The factory where I worked was being evacuated to Siberia where German planes were not yet flying. I was fortunate that I didn't have to go along for I was pregnant, so they did not take me.

I had to walk the fifty kilometers to my mother's village since the trains were occupied with the military. They were happy to see that I was still alive for they had heard rumors of the heavy bombing; but when I related to my mother the reason for my visit, the atmosphere changed abruptly. I told her I wanted to leave my son Arnold with her so that when the time came for delivery I could go to the hospital and not worry about him.

To my surprise, my mother refused; and, no matter how much my sisters and I pleaded with her, she would not change her mind. She stubbornly insisted that my son and I were a family just as she and my sisters were another family. She said I should keep him with me, no matter what happened. I was angry with her, calling her hard-hearted, but nothing would change her mind. She kept saying that no one knew what would happen to all of us, and that she didn't want the responsibility of caring for my son.

So with a heavy heart, not really understanding what motivated her to be so hard for I knew she loved Arnold, I returned to the city the very next day. I was hurt and confused, for I thought she would surely want Arnold to be safe. Going again by foot, carrying my child in my arms or piggyback, we approached the city of Molotchansk. I was surprised to find a strange silence, yes, almost a hush suspended over the whole city. It frightened me a little, but I soon found out that the German army had taken the city in a surprise rush and with very little opposition. The people who had been waiting to be shipped out to Siberia never left. The Reds tried to shoot them when they saw it was *too late to send them to Siberia,* but many good people stopped them. They were finally allowed to go back to their homes, only to find they had been ransacked during their absence. But the people were undaunted for they were happy to be alive.

My landlady and I rejoiced for it seemed the worst was over. The Germans didn't bother us. They were too taken up with the war they still had to fight, and they worried about their families far away at home who were living on meager food stamps, not knowing when the war would end. Here they were fighting in Russia while their homeland was being bombed by Anglo-French planes and later even American

43

planes. It was chaos, and no one laughed about it. When we talked with the regular soldiers, they told us that they weren't happy to be in Russia and even less happy to be fighting a war. They, too, had to be careful about expressing their true feelings, but once in a while one would say that Hitler was a madman.

Chapter 15

WHERE IS MY MOTHER? WHERE ARE MY SISTERS?

After seeing that the Communists had left, I felt it was safe to go back to my mother and sisters. I felt guilty for having left angry and wanted to tell Mom that it was all right and that I forgave her. I didn't know it was too late.

When I entered the first German-Russian village of Klein-Nassau (little Nassau), I found it deserted. There was nothing but dogs, cats and hungry farm animals. So gruesome was the sight that I shivered involuntarily. I pressed on feverishly, driven more by fear than strength. I didn't even notice my weary body, laden with the burden of two children. This was also the month for me to be delivered.

From Klein-Nassau I entered Hochstadt and found the same situation there—no one was left behind. Next I entered Leitershausen and the whole village was in shambles. Kostheim was next. Here we had many relatives and I had hoped to rest overnight in one of their homes, but nobody was there either. Next was Richenfeld and that had the same eerie silence as did all the other towns. Though I feared the worst had happened to all the villages, I still fought fatigue and pressed on once more to Mariaheim. I still hoped to see someone who could tell me what had happened to all the people.

I entered Kronsfeld. I had walked through this village so many times in the past, but today it was different. Everything was dead still. One could cut through the unbearable silence with a knife. Then I faced the last five kilometers to Mariaheim. My heart was beating so fast, I felt it had risen to my throat. I thought I'd die from anxiety as I trod the last few kilometers to Mariaheim. I had mixed emotions about continuing. Though I was eager to keep going, I somehow felt I'd rather turn back, for now it was obvious that every German village in the whole Ukraine was empty. Every person was gone; old, young, children—everyone.

I hoped there would at least be a note from mother, so I continued through the empty streets. These same streets where once I had run and played and danced, where once music had been played and where there once had been laughter despite our half-full stomachs, now they were silent and empty. I never saw a dead body in any of the many empty streets and yet I felt as if I had been to a mass funeral, so dead were the towns. There were no sounds except the occasional barking of a dog. The air seemed to stand still and the leaves hung motionless on their branches.

A thousand questions flowed through my thoughts before I reached the house where I was born. Nothing was drastically changed. The chickens and pigs hadn't been fed for I don't know how long. I trembled as I entered the empty structure. There was no more glass in the windows and the floor boards had been ripped up to be used as firewood.

There was no note to be found anywhere. What was especially strange was that there wasn't an article of clothing to be seen anywhere. I completely forgot about my son and ran upstairs to the attic. I found an old shoe lying on the floor at the top of the stairs. I picked it up and pressed it to my bosom as though it were more precious than gold for it had once been worn by my mother. I kissed that shoe and wept. I demanded an answer from that shoe, "Where is my mother? Where are my sisters? Where has everybody gone?" But the old shoe was just as empty and lonely as I was because the woman who had once worn it was here no more.

I ran to the window and gripped the frame. I screamed so loudly that heaven must have heard me. I lamented that all were gone and I was left behind all alone. I wished I was with them and could share their tragic lot, but I was unwanted—rejected.

As I stood there at the window crying until my eyes burned, I suddenly felt a little tug on my dress and heard a

46

small voice say, "Mommy, don't cry. I am here, I'm with you. You're not alone. I'll take care of you."

"Oh, my God!" I gasped. "Yes, my son. At least you are here. It's just you and me now as a family, just like my mother had said."

The small voice of my child had brought me to my senses. I shuddered now at the thought of what might have happened had my mother kept my child. I would have no one now. So in the midst of what seemed to be an absolute disaster, I realized that the Lord had hardened my mother's heart so that I might now have my son with me in this great empty village, which suddenly had turned into a real ghost town.

Chapter 16

NO TIME FOR GRIEF

So here I was with the potatoes, beets and carrots still in the ground and no one to dig them up but me. I had no time to spare, for fall was upon us and the weather was getting colder every day. I had to hurry to dig the vegetables, otherwise we'd have nothing to eat.

There was no glass in the windows so I had to act quickly to repair them. I had to get a cow from the collective farm, gather chickens together and generally prepare for a hard Russian winter. I went from one of my relatives' houses to another and took what I needed. There was something left in every house, so what I didn't find in one I discovered in the next. I found old sheets for diapers and clothing for the baby. I dragged home beds and matresses. It amazed me to see all that the people had left behind. They must have taken them just the way they were. All I found was in pretty bad shape but even these rags helped.

The German soldiers had not passed through this territory as yet. Only Rumanians, who were allies of the Germans, had been here. The Rumanian culture was very different from ours and they had wrecked much of what the Ukrainians had left behind. They might have made a short stop just to rest and find food because I found a kettle standing on my mother's stove in which they had boiled chicken, or had my mother left it behind? Whoever it had been, they hadn't time to eat it for it nearly sickened me when I lifted the lid. I threw it to the dogs who were hungry enough to eat it.

Every house was dirty, but I only cleaned my parent's house. I fixed the windows and the doors and made it half-way livable. Now it was about time to have my baby, and the realization that I was all alone to deliver terrified me. What would I do? I had never seen a baby being born. How could I help myself? If only I hadn't limited God, He would have sent someone immediately; but I couldn't imagine God caring about what was to take place shortly. On October 21st I went into labor and after a long, agonizing struggle I delivered a baby boy. I knew nothing about umbilical cords so I simply did what came to my mind.

After the baby was born, I had a terrible time getting rid of the afterbirth and would have died if an old Polish woman from a neighboring village had not wandered into Mariaheim. Prior to that she had avoided coming because the village was empty and spooky, but on that particular day she felt she must muster up enough courage to venture in. I was so happy to see her. I told her what had happened. She checked the baby and saw there was nothing she could do for him. He had bled to death because the cord was not clamped properly. She got a box, put my baby into it and buried him. The old woman then took bricks and put them in hot embers. She wrapped them and put them on my abdomen so the warmth would cause my body to expel the afterbirth. I felt so sorry for myself that I had to be alone and that I had lost the baby, but she stopped me immediately by telling me this was no time for self-pity and that I must relax. Finally I did get rid of the afterbirth.

The very next day a hay wagon lumbered through the empty streets. She stopped the driver, asked him where he was headed and begged him to take Arnold and me along. Another miracle was in the making for he was headed toward Molotchansk. The driver agreed to take my little boy and me along on the wagon. Slowly we moved ahead. It was good to cuddle down in the hay and rest. Our clothing was thin so the hay was the welcome warmth we needed.

When we got to the city, I directed him to my in-laws. They received me well and tried to help me, but there really wasn't much to do. They were embarrassed about what they had done to me. I didn't care, for what was past was to be forgotten. I had the future to consider so I stayed briefly and then went to my landlady, who took us in and cared for us.

Things had deteriorated in Molotchansk for the German army took what little food there was and the hound of starvation was at the back door. I had no choice but to take Arnold, a few belongings and return to Mariaheim where at least there was food.

Upon our return I found nothing had changed, it was as empty as before. I worked hard and prepared much more than the two of us needed in the hope that my mother, babushka and sisters would come back, along with all the other friends of my youth. So life went on and I waited day after day for their return. I had no one to talk to but my little boy. At night when he slept, I'd sit by the window and stare out into the darkened street. I had difficulty sleeping at night and could finally only fall asleep for a few hours near morning.

I lived in constant fear for I knew guerilla soldiers were all over the area. I don't really know how many days passed in this way but I remember it was a depressing period, one I'll never forget. One could not even find a footprint in the dusty street. There were no wagons, nothing but silence day after day, and in the night the haunting hooting of the owls. They had built their nests in the chimneys of the empty houses. It seemed that they were crying and calling for the ones who had been carried away into captivity. Those owls really got to me for they pierced through me to the very marrow of my bones. They were driving me to madness. I had to do something about this deplorable situation, but what?

Chapter 17

MY ENCOUNTER WITH THE GERMAN SOLDIERS

One day as my little boy and I were sitting in the kitchen, we heard a clattering noise coming up the street. I grabbed Arnold and ran into the street to see where this noise was coming from. As we stood outside the front gate, a cloud of dust came rolling toward us. It came closer and closer until finally we could see a motorcycle with a wagon attached to its side, and in it were three German soldiers. They were amazed to see that there was life in the village and started to motion to me, thinking I didn't understand German. They were taken by surprise when they heard me speak their language. They asked where all the people from the villages were and I explained what had happened. They then promised me that they'd return to get us. They wanted me to become the interpreter between them and the Ukrainian people. I didn't care to stay in Mariaheim any longer since it was obvious that my people would not return. There was no sense in waiting in this haunted village another day so I agreed to go with them. Besides, it was better to get a ride than to walk.

They did return later to take inventory of what remained behind in Mariaheim. They were far from their homeland so they needed the food that grew in Russia. I was now busy from dawn to dusk for there was much to do and there weren't many interpreters. I was very much in demand. I feared this job would not last long for it was too peaceful.

I now had a housekeeper named Sheny. She was a widow, too, but had no children. She took Arnold to her heart and cared very well for him and me. We were now a family of three. My job as interpreter took me all around the Ukraine but I always returned at night.

51

Though my folks had all disappeared into the unknown and I never heard from them again, I had a peace about it. I accepted the situation for what it was. I couldn't change it, so why fight it? God would take care of it all. Besides, hadn't my father written from his prison that we would never see each other in this world again but only in the world to come? Even though I didn't understand the mystery of God, somehow I understood what my father had said. I knew in my heart that I could not control my future with all its circumstances; so why worry about it? I learned to take one day at a time and enjoy what was good. When a day was unpleasant I'd pretend it had never existed. I'd cancel it out as quickly as possible and not ponder over it but dream of a better day. It seemed a long time went by with that kind of contentment.

But, eventually, the clouds over us began to darken and I sensed things were changing around us. There was more military activity in 1943 than there had been in 1941. There were troops all about us. Reports came about retreats from Caucasus, the precious oil fields and from Stalingrad where the Germans had hoped to command the Volga River along the thousand mile line from the Baltic to the Caspian Sea at Astrakhan. I was merely an interpreter and housewife and not a politician nor of the military, but this was something of great interest to me. I wanted to see Russia freed from Communism. I hoped that our great generals would reform by taking our own Ukrainian boys and defeating both the Communists and the Nazis and freeing us. I didn't want to see the Third Reich's victory. If I leaned any way, it was toward the old Czarist rule, for it had been a good period for my ancestors in Russia. But, alas, it was only a dream and certainly not a possibility.

Twice each year, at the end of October and at the end of March, the roads in Russia became quagmires of mud. The fall rains and spring thaw brought all mechanized warfare to a halt for at least three weeks. This abruptly ended the Russian offensive and left both sides exhausted and gasping for breath.

Though the Germans had committed all their reserves to the effort, they had failed to take Stalingrad. They had thrown everything into that last, desperate thrust but, despite their gallant effort, the Soviet's fresh onslaught was too much for them. In a thunderclap, the entire German sixth army was surrounded. They held out for seven weeks but finally on January 31, 1943, they were out of ammunition, food, fuel and medical supplies. Against the direct order of Hitler (the Führer), what remained of the sixth army surrendered— 91,000 officers and men were taken prisoner and nearly twice that many remained buried in the deep snows of the Russian steppes. To my knowledge, it was the worst defeat in German military history and the turning point of the war. By July we knew that the Germans had lost their war and the curtain was descending on the thousand-year Reich—990 years ahead of schedule. But there was no private rejoicing in the Ukraine. The alternative awaiting us was hardly something to shout about, or even to whisper about.

Chapter 18

REICHENFELD PANIC AND RETREAT—
GOOD-BYE RUSSIA FOREVER

In two years, the Germans had scarcely begun to adapt themselves to the unbelievable extremes of the Russian winter which the Soviet army took as a matter of course. Also, in civilian life the Russian soldier was used to functioning on little or no food, but the Germans had difficulty with this. Just as 130 years before when Napoleon had been overcome and was forced to retreat, so again the greatest ally the Russians had—a hard, cold winter—now forced the Germans to withdraw.

We were told on September 13, 1943 to retreat from Reichenfeld where we were now living. I had no need to be told because I had no intention of staying. If the Reds were unkind to me before, it would be no picnic now when they returned and found I had worked for the Germans as an interpreter. I could just imagine what would happen to me. No thank you, I'd leave. So once again, after a long time, I set my face toward America. I seemed to be closer to my vision than ever before.

My housekeeper Sheny and a refugee from Caucasus by the name of Maxim packed our belongings on the covered wagon (much like the pioneer wagons of the western United States), but it held mostly food. My son rode in the wagon with the driver, but Sheny and I had to walk. We tied two cows to the wagon because we were told by the Germans that we'd return as soon as the Reds were driven back. I didn't believe what they said, nor did I want to believe it at this point. This was my chance to cross the border, a chance I'd never had before and perhaps would not have again. But for the sake of peace and milk on the road for my child and us, I agreed to take the cows. It was fortunate we had them for they provided the only source of food later in our trek.

We were heading for the Perekop Bridge at the south-west end of the Dnieper. We went at a slow pace from sunrise to sundown, never stopping. I don't know how those poor animals could go on for their hooves were split after the first few days. There were so many of us on the road that some-times I felt the road would collapse and swallow us up. We went on and on from one day to another, from one town to another. We didn't care where we were. At least I didn't, for I was happy to be leaving Russia and Communism.

At night we'd sit around a fire and drink warm milk and plan for the next day. The Soviet planes bombed us once in a while and sometimes they would hit somebody or something, but most of the time we kept on moving peacefully until we crossed the Dnieper at the Perekop Bridge. It had to be God's intervention that brought our wagon safely across because the bombing was now very heavy. Limbs from human bodies and animals flew through the air. It seemed the bombs just brushed past us at times. The Russians had hoped to stop us at this strategic point, but many lived through the bombing and got across the river.

Finally, after weeks on the road, we were ordered to stop at Bastanovka, a place not far from Krivoj Rog (an iron-producing area) and Nikolajev. Here we were to rest up for the remainder of the journey.

While we camped there another girl, an interpreter like myself, and I decided to take the risk and break away from the wagon train; take a train and go to Nikolajev. My father had told me it was a beautiful city and he hoped I'd get to see it some day. It was indeed a beautiful city, perhaps the most beautiful one in the whole Ukraine. It was so clean and trim with its lovely trees along the streets. It was a sight to behold. Nikolajev was named after the Czar Nikolay and I'm surprised that the Communists did not rename this city as they had so many others after the Revolution.

55

We had taken a chance slipping off to Nikolajev because we didn't know how long we were to camp in Bastanovka. If the wagon train had left, I would have been separated from Sheny and Arnold. But we did return on time and I saw a beautiful side of Russia before leaving.

From that time on, only terror and struggle were our daily fare. We feared for our lives constantly, not only from visible enemies but from invisible ones who were the worst. They were the partisans or guerillas.

We moved slowly through the Umam Forest and Pervomaysk, driving uphill most of the time in mud almost up to our ankles. It was October, and there wasn't one day without rain. Sheny and I had to constantly push the rear wheels out of the mud. Our strength nearly gave out at times, but we moved on as fast as we could throughout each day. However, it was the danger of the night that we had to fear most of all.

Many times people would go in the fields nearby to get some hay or straw for our poor horses and cows and would not return again. The partisans would kill them. They were now all around us—in the forests, on trains, everywhere. They were dressed in civilian clothes, so it was difficult to tell who they were.

In Uman we were regrouped. Women with children were loaded on trains but the others had to continue on foot and wagons, a trip that was suicidal. My poor friend and companion, Sheny and Maxim from Caucasus, had to continue on the wagon train. My son and I were put on the train without anything except what we had on us. It was a small train that only went on narrow tracks. The train was cold and damp; and when we tried to talk our teeth chattered. We were poorly dressed for this cold weather. If this train would be able to take us to Poland we would not have to travel many months to get there; but nothing went right. The devil didn't want us to get out of his Communistic hell, so he was constantly blocking our path. As soon as one roadblock was removed, another would lie ahead. Then when we attempted to cross the railroad bridge from Uman into Vinnitso, our train was dynamited and every car in front of ours was blown up by the explosion. Ours, the last car, suddenly came to a stop just before it would have plunged into the deep gully below. It was as if thousands of angels had held it back.

When we realized what had happened, we took a head count; and to this day I haven't forgotten that number. We were fifty-eight women and children in that car. I was the only one with one child. The others had three or four children. We climbed out of the train and looked over our situation. We were about one kilometer from a small depot which was just a signal station for trains. But we went there and carried our children, one by one, away from the rubble to safety.

Our children were very cold so we laid ourselves down over them to protect them from the cold and to warm their little bodies. But what could we feed them? We were now in the valley and we would have to climb up the hills to find food. The man at the depot had told us that there were people in the hills, but they were infiltrated with partisans and they'd kill us on sight. He said that the week before a caravan had come through and sought refuge overnight in a nearby barn. Out of nowhere shooting started and bullets ripped through the walls. Everybody was killed or taken prisoner. No one knew for sure what happened to them; it was a frightful sight, he said. Now the villagers didn't communicate with anyone anymore for they feared for their lives.

So we had a new problem to solve. I was no hero, but I was desperate. Live or die, I couldn't bear to linger on without doing something; so I decided to take a chance. I called the women around me and told them something had to be done and that I was going to try to get help. If they killed me, they'd have just one more child to take care of. There was little hope, but I preferred to take this chance rather than sitting and waiting. I found some bandages and bandaged my face and head, except for one eye. I got an old basket and hung it over my arm, pretending to be an old woman looking for firewood. I climbed up from the valley, about fifty or sixty feet above, went around and crossed another bridge for wagons and trucks. I couldn't believe it for, so far, no one stopped me. I walked through a little forest and soon entered Rumanian occupied territory where, for some reason, there were no partisans.

I went straight to the officer in charge, told him our problem and how many of us there were. He immediately called for a five-ton truck with guards and put me on it. We went back for the fifty-eight women and children, including my son Arnold. For us there was joy, there was victory. You can't imagine how happy we were to be rescued from our unfortunate plight.

The truck took us to the next city which was Proskurov. We arrived there at night. I don't recall too well what the city was like, but I will remember for the rest of my life how hospitable the people were to us. We were brought to a hotel, had a wonderful bath, food and a real bed. After two months on the road it was a welcome sight, to be sure. It is well to remember that it really doesn't take much to make a weary traveler happy. Oh, how good it felt to rest our tired bodies and to have a warm meal, even if the food was poor!

Chapter 19

THE FIGHT FOR RELEASE AND THE ENTRY INTO CZECHOSLOVAKIA

The German commanding officer of the city of Proskurov didn't want to allow me to cross the border from West Ukraine into Poland. But I would not take "no" for an answer. I went back to him every day for a week. He threw me out the back door and I returned through the front door. The problem was that I was listed as an interpreter and he didn't want to let me out of the country. I told him I was not a soldier in his army but a mother who had to get her child to safety. If he didn't give me a passport, I'd go anyway. As far as I was concerned, the war was over. I had left my birthplace, set my face toward America and only a bullet could stop me now. He finally realized I wasn't kidding but meant every word I said, so he gave in and I got a passport for my son and myself.

The next day we were loaded into animal cars on the train to Lvov, Poland. There was no more bombing and the only times we stopped were to eat something and then we would continue the journey once again.

We were so packed in those cars that we almost sat on top of one another; so if anyone had lice, everyone got them. We were so infested with lice that we scratched continually. By the end of the trip our bodies were sore and bleeding from scratching.

When we got to Lvov we were forced to go through a disinfectant station. Then we were transferred to another train and immediately sent to Teplitz Shönau in western Czechoslovakia, where we arrived on December 19, 1943.

After a few days we were acclimated to our new home.

It was a big school which had been converted into a camp for refugees of all nationalities from Eastern Europe.

One morning as I left the building, I got so dizzy I had to hold on to the railing. Everything turned dark in front of my eyes, and that was the last I remember. A Red Cross worker found me on the ground and held me at the camp for observation, but the fever I had didn't break. On Christmas Eve, 1943, they brought me to a Catholic hospital supervised by the Sisters of the Holy Cross.

I was in a white bed with clean linen and gentle sisters were standing around my bed singing Christmas carols. As I opened my eyes, I thought I had already died and was in heaven. In fact, when one of the sisters in white bent over me to check how I was, I asked her, "Am I in heaven?" She said, "No, you're in a hospital."

Shortly after, I was sent to an isolated building and one sister cared for me all the time. I had such a high fever that I spent long periods in delirium. For short intervals I'd regain consciousness to find a nun sitting next to my bed. "What is the matter with me?" I'd ask. "And who are you?" She answered, "You have typhoid fever and I am Sister Annayana. I'm taking care of you because I had typhoid fever myself."

When she first told me, I remember how upset I was about Arnold's whereabouts. Who would care for him, and how long would I have to be in the hospital? When she told me I'd have to be there until all the tests were negative, which would take at least six weeks, I flew into a rage and had to be restrained from trying to get out of bed.

Chapter 20

AT DEATH'S DOOR

I had more comfort in that hospital than I had ever known in all my life, a good bed, all the food in the world (if I only had an appetite) and the most compassionate nun one could imagine in Sister Annayana. If you knew Jesus, you could not help but see Him in her. She was in her fifties, always dressed in a white veil and robe with a large cross on her chest. That alone made me feel tremendous love and respect for her.

She never asked me whether I believed in God or to what denomination I belonged. She just labored unceasingly and cared for the sick in this whole building without complaining or grumbling. She always had a smile and a gentle touch to accompany it. It was too overwhelming for me, for I had almost never received love in my life. I accepted this attention with a trembling heart and gladly returned that love, but never said so in words. I just wanted her always in my room, for I felt so secure when she was near. She never asked questions, but I had many. I wanted to know who she was, what nationality and so on. She patiently answered them all. She was Sudeten-German. Her ancestors had immigrated from the Alpine section of Bavaria about the same time my people had immigrated from Württemberg. Sister Annayana had always been sickly as a child. She loved the Lord and so she felt the call to the religious order of the Holy Cross. This I had difficulty understanding, but her voice was so soothing to my spirit that I just lay there and listened to her. It held such compassion that one could not help but know that what she was saying about loving the Lord must be true because she personified that love to others.

Most of the time I lay in bed enjoying the sunshine that flooded my room. It was a very pleasant room, and I did not mind resting there after so many years of toil and tragedy. In this building cases of infectious illnesses such as polio or typhus were confined. After three weeks I was told that I was out of danger since the high fever that had burned my body for so long had finally subsided.

One bright sunny morning Sister Annayana announced that she was going to take me to the bathroom for a bath. Since I had only had sponge baths throughout my illness, it was necessary. She treated me like a child throughout this experience, and rightly so, for where I came from I had never seen a bathroom like this. But to my dismay, I got worse after the bath. That very night I awoke with the feeling that someone had stuck pins and needles into my chest. As I reached for the bell near my bed, the pain was so excruciating that I cried aloud. When Sister Annayana came in, she knew something was very wrong and, upon examining me and asking for symptoms, she diagnosed the illness as pleurisy.

When Dr. Kukutch came by on his rounds a few hours later, he ordered x-rays which confirmed Sister Annayana's diagnosis. From then on I was in constant pain; it felt as though my chest were on fire. I didn't know what medication I was getting, but now I know it was morphine.

The pain was excruciating. I lay on an air mattress but I couldn't lift my head off the pillow, so they set up a frame-like device with a sling hanging from it and placed it directly overhead. This way I could hold onto the sling with my hands when they turned me or wanted to lift my body.

I entered the hospital in December and remained in bed for nineteen weeks. I would never have believed that any person could lie in bed for so long, much less myself. I was used to moving around and couldn't sit still. Usually I could do something to get out of a predicament, but this time was different. I couldn't even feed myself; I had to rely on others.

And I couldn't take care of my son; he was being cared for at the refugee camp by Ukrainian people who took him in as if he were their own son. Often the Red Cross Sister would bring him to see me through the glass door. He understood that he could not come into my room, for he spoke Ukrainian fluently and was now learning to speak German as well. One week they did not bring him to visit me and I just knew something was wrong. I asked the nun to check on him for me, but she always said he was all right. Finally they brought him to see me and I was terribly shocked, for his head was all bandaged.

They explained how he had been playing with the other children and had been accidently pushed against a large radiator in the hallway, striking his head against it. A large gash above his right eye spurted blood. Fortunately, the wound was not lower for he could have lost his eye. I heard Sister Annayana thanking God and I joined in because it could have been so much worse.

Most of the time I lay there in my bed with nothing to do but think. I had much time to reflect on all that had happened since 1941 when I saw my sisters and mother for the last time. I thought about my whole life and began to feel very sorry for myself. I thought of how I had never really been a child, nor a teenager. It seemed I had never been young or with carefree thoughts of youth. Then I began to see that my hard life as a child had prepared me for the long trek out of Russia. Had I had a soft life, I would have been buried along with so many others at the roadside, and what would have happened to my child then? And what if I had not made it to safety before becoming sick? No one would have cared for me on the road. I came to the realization that my misfortunes had turned to blessings in most cases. But here I was in the midst of trouble once again. I was in such pain and it seemed I'd never get better. How long was this going to continue?

Then one morning while on his rounds, Dr. Kukutch came in and Sister Annayana complained that I constantly begged for more medicine. Dr. Kukutch very calmly said to her, "Give her all she wants. Her lungs are filled with fluid so don't let her suffer. She's not going to make it anyhow, so try and keep her comfortable."

"I am going to die," I thought to myself. "I'm glad; it will soon be all over. Then there will be no more suffering, no more starvation, no more freezing, no more pushing wagons. This is the end of the line. Why not? I have nobody except my son and someone will surely adopt him. He's a good boy and will please someone." All these thoughts ran quickly through my mind.

Then Sister Annayana came to my bedside and asked if I had heard what the doctor said. I answered, "Yes, I heard." And quickly added, "I'm glad it'll soon be over; now I will get some rest."

But she looked worried and asked if I knew God, if I had been baptized, what faith I professed, if any. It was the first time anyone had ever asked me what faith I was, and it was a tough question for me to answer. I explained I was baptized as a baby by a visiting Polish priest, Father Mokelke, but that was all. She said that's all she needed to know and disappeared.

When she returned she was not alone. She brought a priest with her and then left us alone. Though I don't remember his name, he was a kind elderly priest. He immediately asked if I had any sins to confess. I answered that I had very many. He heard my confession and helped me at every step. We got along just fine. Then he said he'd give me my first holy communion. He asked me to repeat after him, "Lord Jesus, come into my heart." I repeated those words and received my first communion. Then he took a little jar, opened it and came nearer to my bed and said, "I am going to give you the last rights of the church (now more rightfully called 'the sacrament of healing'). When you die, you'll go to heaven, my child."

For the first time in a long while I was happy. I didn't think of anyone, not even my child. All I could think of was how it would be in heaven. I thought and thought of that until I fell asleep. I slept right through the night. Not once did

I ring the bell all night long.

In the morning the bright May sun flowed into my room. Shortly after I awoke, Sister Annayana came rushing into my room, expecting to find me dead for she, too, was able to sleep uninterrupted throughout the night and had not heard my bell. Instead of finding me dead, I was very much alive and hungry for the first time in nineteen weeks. When I asked for food, her face lit up and she said, "You can have whatever you want!"

When you are a farmer's daughter from Russia, your taste buds are not very refined so I asked for salt pork and raw onions. She gasped and said, "But that will kill you!" But she did bring me what I asked for and it didn't kill me!

Chapter 21

GOD'S MIRACULOUS HELP FOR ME AND MY SON

I was instantly healed, and my healing was even greater than I realized at the time. When I came to America I found out about withdrawal from drugs, and only then did I realize what the Lord had done for me. Not only did He heal me, but He took all desire for morphine away from me; for after nineteen weeks I had certainly become addicted. That was the fear Sister Annayana had expressed to Dr. Kukutch when he said I was going to die.

I had to have all sorts of x-rays taken. I wanted to go to my son right away; but Dr. Kukutch and Sister Annayana insisted that I get my strength back, which didn't seem to be a problem at all. In no time I was as good as new. The x-rays showed only two scars where they had punctured my lungs to draw out the fluid. (By the time I came to America even these two scars had disappeared. Otherwise, I could not have entered the States. Isn't God good!)

While I was recuperating, Sister Annayana was taking me to the chapel where Father John Newmann was instructing me in my faith. Of all the things he taught me, the fact that impressed me the most was that the Holy Spirit had overshadowed the Virgin Mary and she had conceived the child who was the Son of God, Jesus Christ. One might think I could not comprehend this, but I did. It seemed very simple to me. It hit me like a bolt of lightning and stayed with me until now. No one can realize how much this same Holy Spirit continually instructed, guided and even strengthened me for the great trials that still lay ahead of me.

Soon I was released. My son and I were sent to Eastern Bohemia (Sudetenland). This time they put us in a monastery, the home of the Sisters of Mercy. They gave us a home for as long as we needed, and it was welcomed and appreciated. We stayed three weeks. We had a good time climbing Alt Vater Berg (Old Father Mountain).

The village was called Einsiedel. It is called Alt Vater Gebeurge in German. The entire population there were German immigrants.

After three weeks, restlessness set in. I told the Mother Superior that I wanted to find work, and she agreed with me. So I went to the unemployment office and immediately got a job in Freudenthal (Joy Valley), near Tropau. I was hired to work in the railroad office doing the payroll for all the workers. The girl whose job I was taking, Rose Spindler, was supposed to train me for this work.

She went over it time and time again until she was blue in the face, but still I could not understand the worksheet. I felt like a blockhead. Since she was to have a baby any time, I decided to tell them to get someone else because I just couldn't do the work. But before I did, I remembered Father Newmann's lesson on the Holy Spirit. So I decided to pray to Him. I simply said, "Holy Spirit, if You were so powerful that You overshadowed the Virgin Mary and she became with child, You most certainly can enlighten me and teach me how to do this work."

The next morning I got up and went to the office. I didn't feel any smarter, but when Rose went over the routine again, lo and behold, a light went on in my head. I immediately asked to do it. She just stared at me at first, but then gave me the pencil. I did the work perfectly. I knew my childish prayer had been answered.

The next problem facing me was finding a place to live. I couldn't possibly leave my son at the monastery all day and commute by train, so I started to look for a place to stay near my work. But no one wanted us. Everyone slammed the door in my face with the remark, "Go away, you lousy Russian!" I cried, "Oh no, not again!" In Russia we were "German pigs" and now "lousy Russians." What next? If only I could go to America now. But it wasn't God's time yet. This was only a rest stop and we would move on when the time was right.

For the time being, my son and I slept in the office where I worked. My son spent his days in kindergarten where he was well taken care of, especially after what we were used to. At night we'd push the desks together, roll out a mattress and sleep on it. Fortunately there was a bathroom. In the morning Arnold would go to school and I would put everything back in its place before the other workers arrived.

Soon a big factory owner named Machhold offered us a room with adjoining bath for which we were happy and grateful. We didn't need much, for on weekends we visited our adopted family, the Sisters of Mercy. How Arnold and I looked forward to that visit! The train ride was so delightful as we admired the majestic pine trees on each side of the train.

On one of these trips we sat in a cabin with two women and a child. Their names were Mizzi and Hidelies Schoeber. We were having a very interesting conversation. They were such friendly people that I was deeply engrossed in what we were talking about. Suddenly everyone around us cried out and gasped in shock. I turned around to see what it was that they were so upset about. My heart nearly stopped when I saw the conductor holding my son by the shirt, pulling him back into the train.

Those watching said I hadn't seen the worst, for Arnold was about to fall off the train when this man caught him a split second before it would have been too late, and had saved his life. I cried at the realization that Arnold had nearly been killed. Again, I would have been alone. What a scare that child gave me and everybody else on the train!

I became good friends with these two women. They gave me their address and on our return we visited them for they lived in Freudenthal.

Meanwhile I was still corresponding with Sister Annayana and Father Newmann. One day Father John's letter was returned with the information on it that he had died. I felt lost without him for he was my first spiritual guide and I needed much guidance. "Oh, God," I asked, "why do I lose everybody?"

Chapter 22

THE BOMB THAT NEVER EXPLODED

For a while everything was very routine. I heard a lot of complaints from the Czechs and Bohemian Germans about the food and clothing rations; but we never complained for it was much better than what we had had in Russia. Even though we had food rations, we at least knew we'd be able to get our food without waiting in long lines. We had always had so little that what we now had in Bohemia seemed a lot. I now had two coats, two pair of shoes and one time somebody left a pair of golden sandals at the door of my room. To this day I don't know where they came from. They were even the right size; I was so proud of them.

The whole building where I lived was filled with war widows. Mrs. Jacobs was next to me, Mrs. Nitche was across the hall from me. The three of us had to share the bathroom, but there was never any trouble. We got along very well. Neither of these women had children. Only I had Arnold, and he became everybody's darling. He was always "at home" anywhere and nothing bothered him as long as he had food.

We were doing well in the food department now. We had our rations and we even had extras. Mrs. Nitche was a cook at the Machhold factory. She brought food for Arnold that he never tasted before like rice, cocoa, chocolate and cream of wheat. He loved the latter and so did I, but it was brought for Arnold.

My best girlfriend from Caucasus was Inge Reunstadt. She was Jewish, but only she and I knew that. Everybody thought she was German because she had her papers changed when she escaped from Caucasus. We had worked together as interpreters before our escape.

Inge was the finest pianist I had ever heard. When we escaped we were separated, but later through the Red Cross we were reunited. She now worked in the office of a bakery in Niederschlesien (lower Silesia) in Glogau. She was also an excellent bookkeeper. They were happy to have her and no one questioned her papers. Since she worked for the bakery, Arnold and I had it made! She supplied us with bread stamps so we never went hungry for as long as we were in Freudenthal.

But something happened one night that shook the whole building where we lived. That night I had brought home work from the office, as always. We were short of help and I never seemed to have enough hours in which to get the work done. I darkened the room with blankets at the window so nobody would see the light. It was punishable by law if we did not have blackout in our rooms at night.

So that particular night I worked late and then went to bed for I was very tired. My bed was across from the coal stove which stood against the wall. My son's crib stood next to the door. In the middle of the room was a table with two chairs. It was sparsely furnished and even these were borrowed. No sooner had I gone to bed when the whole house shook. I was so covered with ashes from the stove that I looked like a chimney sweep. But, other than that, everything seemed fine. Next we heard a loud knocking at our door. It all happened so fast that I didn't realize what was happening. I ran to the door. Meanwhile Arnold had awakened and was crying with fear.

I opened the door and there stood every woman from the house, plus a policeman. They all thought we were dead. I was surprised and asked why. They took me aside and showed me the hole right behind the wall of our room. A bomb had dropped down there and was stuck in the cellar. It never went off, so everybody was safe. My stove was the only casualty, for all the pressure from behind it had blown it out. In spite of the fact that we almost got killed, we all laughed. That was the first bombing by the Russians in Freudenthal

71

and, once again, God had saved us.

Again we went about our daily routine. I enjoyed my work, especially since I now knew the Lord had provided this job and the Holy Spirit had taught me how to do it. What more could I ask, except to have it stay this way for it was quite peaceful.

Chapter 23

THE RUSSIAN ARMY ARRIVES

Isn't it strange how we start searching for God and the churches fill up when trouble strikes? No matter when I'd go to church at this time in Freudenthal, it would be filled to the rafters.

The Germans had retreated, not only from Russian territory but also from Poland. With each day the people grew more and more panicky, and so did I. The Russians were getting closer all the time.

Where would I go now? I had met a German soldier from the Ukraine who had asked me to marry him and had given me his parents' address in Saxony. I corresponded with his mother, but how could I go and burden those people? How I dreaded to flee again, but I had to. I could not possibly stay and wait until the advancing Russian army occupied this city. Yet, because of the importance of the railroad I couldn't leave until I was allowed to leave by my boss. I didn't want to desert him.

So I stuck it out until the city fathers hung out the white flag as a sign that they wouldn't fight but would surrender the city peacefully. Little did they know what kind of *peace* they'd have as a result of Russian occupation.

So at the last minute I took my son Arnold and ran as fast as I could to the railroad station. I asked for passage on a train out of Freudenthal to Saxony, Germany. I was told that the only passage I could get was on a Red Cross transport with 630 wounded soldiers. I would also have to assist the doctors and nurses in caring for the soldiers. I accepted passage and the responsibility of helping. My son sat in a corner and I moved from one car to another wherever I was needed.

So here we were on the road again, surrounded with trouble.

Each kilometer we gained throughout the day would be lost by night as the Czechoslovakian railroad personnel cooperated with the Russians in order to be in favor with them when they marched in. They wanted the Russians to capture us on the day of capitulation so they kept us in Czech territory.

On May 9th the Russian soldiers surrounded our train. I was petrified that someone might betray me, that I had come from Russia. I feared I'd be arrested as a traitor to the Communist cause. I quickly tore up my papers and pictures into shreds and flushed them down the toilet. I won the first round, but the next round wasn't as easy.

Woe to anyone an Asian Russian gets hold of! The European Russian is much more cultured and compassionate. We were surrounded by Asian Russians, and when they fell on the train they looted every car of anything of value—medicine, bandages, the boots of the wounded, pocket knives, playing cards, absolutely everything within sight and reach. Needless to say, the sign of the Red Cross on the train meant nothing to them. They just went berserk. Nobody spoke Russian so they took total advantage of the situation.

Finally one of the nurses got away. She knew that I spoke the Russian language and came in search of me. She found me and pleaded with me to help them. So I went, for how could I refuse? I went right up to them and asked if these things they had taken were of interest to them since there really wasn't anything worth taking. I pleaded with them to leave the poor, broken soldiers alone for they were already half dead. They were startled that I spoke Russian! It's always easier to loot when no one understands you, but this was the last thing they expected. Their first reaction was to drop everything; but then they started asking questions. How did I know how to speak such good Russian? I could not tell them the truth for they would kill me, so I quickly replied that my mother was a Russian and had married my German father. She had taught me to speak Russian. Most of them believed me, but one kept insisting that something was fishy because I spoke better Russian than he did. Asians never speak very good Russian and that seemed to be bothering him. The rest of the men talked him out of his suspicion and they all left together.

Everybody was glad when they left, but little did we realize that they'd return that very night. They made a revengeful attack. They first took the nurses out into the fields and raped them. When the doctors came to their defense, they took them, stripped them and beat them half to death and then left them there.

They then came for me. Two men pulled me out of the wagon. I got away from them and ran into the station, but the railroad officials slammed the door in my face and refused to let me in. I was pleading with them to help me, but to no avail. There I stood with them pulling on my arms, each from a different direction. There was a light pole in front of the railroad station and for a split second I got my arms free from the Reds and threw them quickly around the pole. I had no intention of letting go. I knew what would happen to me if I went with them. So I decided they could kill me right there in front of the train. They kept hitting me all over with butts of their guns, again and again until my face and head were bruised and bleeding.

Finally I realized this wasn't getting me anywhere and something had to be done. I turned my eyes to the Lord and in my heart I whispered, "Jesus, help me." At that same moment I felt strength and courage I didn't know I had. I let my arms down from the pole and, like little David, I hit "Goliath" smack in the nose. Then I hit the other and they both lay on the ground, knocked out.

One thing I did know, I had to disappear fast before they regained consciousness, so I quickly slipped under the train and ran out into the fields. I hid in the bushes along the tracks.

As I lay there, several Russian soldiers came toward the bushes with suitcases full of loot they had confiscated from the train. I was numb with fear. I stopped breathing. My mind was running feverishly. What would I do now? I didn't dare to breathe so I just thought, "Jesus, help me. Jesus, help me." The soldiers placed the loaded suitcases in front of the bushes but didn't see me. The Lord must have blinded them.

As soon as they left, I was panic-stricken for my son's life for he was still on the train. What if they found out he was mine? I had to take another chance. I had to get back on that train!

Chapter 24

A ONE-DAY TRIP THAT LASTED A MONTH AND A HALF

Holding my shoes in my hand, I quietly entered the last car of the train. A Russian soldier was just leaving through the other door of the car but he didn't notice me. I breathed a sigh of relief and thanked God for His protection. I asked the first person I saw, "Where is Arnold?" The nurse replied, "He's safe. The Reds didn't even see him." The answer brought joy to my heart. As the sun peeped over the hills, the train moved out of the railroad station. The realization that most of the occupants of the train were safe filled our beings with wonder and thanksgiving.

I learned many lessons during this ordeal, but one proved profitable later, for I vowed to resort to my "old woman" dress until we were out of Czechoslovakia. Soon after, we were stopped at another train station by the Reds. Two soldiers entered our car and upon seeing me one disgustedly remarked, "Oh, it's just a stara baba (old woman)," and immediately departed. I was never bothered again, though our ordeal was far from over.

We had been left with 630 wounded soldiers, plus doctors and nurses, and without food or medical supplies we desperately needed. At every stop we had to bury our dead in mass graves. All we had for food was oxtail soup which was not very filling and it, too, soon ran out. My son, as little as he was, understood our plight for he never asked for food, sparing me the agonizing necessity of saying that we had none. I was grateful for that, but even his silence was painful.

It was only a short distance from Aussig, Czechoslovakia to the capitol city of Saxony, which is Dresden; and yet we were on the train for a month and a half. I went begging for food at nearly every station. Sometimes I met kind and helpful Czech soldiers who were allies of the Russians. On one occasion a high-ranking police officer listened to my plea for help. He sent a group of his soldiers with me to help carry the supplies he so generously gave us for the whole transport train. It wasn't enough to last until we reached our destination, but it was enough for another day. We were learning not to look ahead to the next day but just to be happy that each person had something in his empty stomach each day. I never saved anything for the next day, not even for my son. He had to learn to control his hunger just as the rest of us did.

When I was in that desperate situation where we thought only of survival, I'd go from house to house begging for others. I never withheld what I received from anybody because they did not believe as I did or were of a different color or nationality. God gave me His compassion and love for each one alike. If He hadn't, I would have broken down with grief or horror because of our sad circumstances. But there was no time for that. Our Lord is a God of action and many times I would take chances for all of us, trusting in His protection. Sometimes I was mistreated and other times I received kindness from those I approached. But as I look back now, I am grateful for both reactions and wouldn't have it any other way. I know that God has a plan for every one of His children and it includes both good and what appears to be bad for "all that happens to us is working for our good if we love God and are fitting into his plans"* (Romans 8:28). I also believe that no matter where that plan starts or ends, or on which soil, it makes little difference to God for "the earth is His footstool" (Matthew 5:35), and He is "the Alpha and the Omega, the Beginning and the Ending of all things"* (Revelation 1:8).

---

*Living Bible

Chapter 25

THE ARRIVAL, DISAPPOINTMENT AND TRIALS
IN SAXONY, GERMANY

In mid-June we arrived at Dresden, once the beautiful capitol of that state. Now it was completely destroyed by bombs. But next to the central station was a Lutheran church still intact. It stood majestically, inviting us to enter. Everyone from the train able to walk marched directly to the church to thank God for being alive. Many fell down on their hands and knees to kiss the floor of that church of God. It was an awesome moment in the presence of our Creator and Savior.

Shortly thereafter, my son and I parted with our comrades of so long, for the Red Cross transport was heading in a different direction than us. We hopped on a coal train going to Kempnitz, which was occupied by the Russians. We kept out of sight, found a place to stay overnight and early the next morning, still dressed in my babushka outfit, started out to Zwickau and then to Werdau, Saxony. This time we were traveling on foot again, though my feet were still swollen from being up continually day and night, helping to care for the soldiers. Nevertheless, we slowly continued our trek.

Naturally we had no food, so we stopped at farms along the way. I would work a day or so to earn enough food and then we'd be on our way again. It was not one of our hardest journeys because we constantly moved along, but we were always on guard. We avoided traffic for fear of the Russians and traveled through fields and back roads. Werdau was occupied by the U.S. Army at that time and we knew we would be safe once we got there.

I don't remember how many days we were on the road or how long it took to get to Zwickau and then to Werdau.

All I do know is that I can still feel the release I felt upon arriving at Zwickau. Immediately I noticed a different atmosphere and we felt secure for the first time in a long while.

I mentioned that I had met a soldier from Werdau back in the Ukraine, so my son and I were traveling to his parents' house. (For security's sake I cannot reveal their names because they still live under Communism in East Germany.) Though we'd never met, I had corresponded with them and they were happy to receive us. We all liked one another immediately. Arnold and I had a *proper* bath for the first time in months. We had a good meal and for the time being were happy once again. Thank God, we didn't think ahead to tomorrow or what that would bring.

The next day the mother of my young soldier friend Herbert called me out to introduce me to a young woman named Irma, who was Herbert's fiancee. I thought the ground would give way from under me for Herbert had promised to marry me. Quickly I accepted defeat. I said to myself, "Why not? I'm a widow with a child. I am a foreigner. Irma is younger, has never been married, is childless and is from the same city. She's a true German while I am a Russian-German." I felt so inferior I was ready to run out of the house, but where would I go? I had to keep quiet and act normal. I couldn't tell Herbert's parents that their son had promised to marry me. Thank God, I had never written about this in my letters to them. I kept it a secret now, too.

Two days later I went to a village near Werdau and found a job. I helped an elderly, childless couple take care of their little farm. I worked for food and a room for Arnold and myself. I did everything; I'd split wood, milk cows, plow the fields, care for the horses, plant crops; I took care of anything that needed attention. The lady of the house did all the work inside with whatever help my son could give.

I remember chopping wood one day and asking God if this was why He brought me out of slavery. I felt so utterly alone. I could not see myself doing this for the rest of my life. But these thoughts weighed me down so that I stopped thinking of the next day and went back to my well-formed habit of taking only one day at a time. This way of thinking made things tolerable and even pleasant at times.

The Kuhlmans were pleased with my services and were generous in helping me to supply Herbert's parents with chickens, eggs, potatoes and what they had. Most Germans were starving after the war, but the farmers had their own produce and normally got on quite well. I was grateful to be working, so no job was degrading as long as it was honest work and we were being fed.

Chapter 26

ATTEMPTED SUICIDE LEADS TO CONCENTRATION CAMP

As I look back through the years, I thank God for His infinite wisdom in leading us from beginning to the end. As my story unfolds you will see clearly that it would have been a disaster if I had become Herbert's wife.

One morning in July of 1945, at 3:00 a.m., I was awakened by the sound of music. I could have enjoyed one more hour of sleep, but on fully awakening I realized what kind of music I was hearing. It was Russian music. More specifically, they were playing the Russian anthem. I thought I was having a nightmare. But no, I was wide awake and ran to the window in order to hear better. It was a nightmare, all right, but I was not sleeping. I was shocked with the realization that the Americans had withdrawn under the cover of darkness and the Russians had taken over Saxony. I was filled with horror and wanted to jump out of the window to the ground below. I wanted to die and die quickly. I looked back at my sleeping son who, in his innocence, did not know what had transpired during the night. I didn't feel strong enough in myself to face the inevitable, but looking over at my growing son I decided we'd face this together and trust in God this time, too. Needless to say, there was no more sleep for me that night. I rushed downstairs to my employers who had already been alarmed. Our security from the American occupation was gone in a split second. The curtain had fallen again. The line of demarkation between the Russians and the Americans had changed. The Russians now had more territory, more people under their Communistic regime and more slaves for their godless, satanic way of life. We soon found

82

out how trapped and helpless we were.

By the time daybreak came, the Red soldiers started their house-to-house looting. They took everything—food, clothing, bicycles, etc. Reports came from all around about raping, and every parent hid his daughter in the cellar or wherever she might be saved from the ravaging. No one and nothing was secure any longer.

The Commander of Werdau came with his guards to pick up Arnold and me in order that I could work for him as a translator. He had learned from the city records that I was from Russia. I was not alone for there were two women from Lithuania who also spoke fluent German and Russian, as well as the Commander's mistress. The Russians provided our food and clothing, but no one enjoyed it. We felt we were being fattened for the kill!

One day a high G.P.U. officer, a colonel, came to get a translator for his organization. I wanted no part of him, but I had no say. Of all the girls, I was chosen.

The first thing my new boss, Colonel Resnik, did was to ask me about my former boss, Gamarov. I thought it was a trap but it turned out later that the G.P.U. really were after him. In fact, later he was arrested, brought to Dresden, stripped of his rank and eventually executed.

The building where my son and I were now housed was under heavy guard so we could not have escaped. We were given a room and a bath common to the soldiers near the kitchen. It wasn't bad except I knew it would not remain that way and I lived in constant fear. Night after night they brought in German men and women for interrogation. Most of these people were well-educated people of great wealth. The interrogations were horrible. My fear drove me to near insanity. I could not forget what had happened to my father, my uncles, my sisters, brother, mother and babushka. They were using me to translate the same demanding accusations. All I could think of was what would happen to me when I was no longer of use to them.

It was this constant fear that drove me across the hall

83

from my room one night after midnight into the office of one of the interrogators. I withdrew a pistol from the desk drawer where I knew he kept it, put the gun to my heart and pulled the trigger.

I expected to die and have peace, but to my horror I was not even unconscious. I just lay there in my blood and in terrible pain until morning. When the First Lieutenant came into the room, he found me and called for an ambulance.

They took me to a German hospital and placed me under guard. The doctors operated and removed all the rib splinters around the wound and sewed me up. The bullet was lodged in my chest, where it remains even to this day as a constant reminder that I had allowed my problems and my circumstances to get bigger than my God. I found out the hard way that God is bigger than anything, even death. I know now that I cannot die until it is God's time.

While recuperating I could not imagine what punishment awaited me. God knew what my future was for He had planned it. Psalm 37:23 says, "The steps of a righteous man are ordered by the Lord."

The secret police came to take me from the hospital. They had my son and all my belongings with them. When we drove off, they were not heading toward the city of Werdau, but instead were taking an unknown road. A cold shiver went over me as I scrutinized the stern, silent faces of the men.

First they brought me to Resa on the Elbe River, a concentration camp. From there we were sent to Oshatz, a KZ[1] camp also on the Elbe River. This concentration camp once held prisoners of war, but when the Americans came they emptied all camps and freed the captives. Now the Russians turned around and were refilling them all. They imprisoned 60,000 of all nationalities, but mostly workers from the Ukraine, Poles and Germans. Men and women were in the same room. It was cold and there was no food nor work. One good thing was that I had Arnold with me, which was more

---

[1]KZ—concentration camp

than I expected from them.

I could see no light in all this darkness. All my hopes were gone. It didn't make sense to me that I had come this far and the Lord was permitting this evil, this satanic power to destroy all my dreams. It was impossible to understand God's ways and yet He was working even in all these circumstances for us.

When I first saw this quiet, pale-faced young man, my heart felt light just being near him. Here I was in the midst of terrible sights and deplorable existence and yet seeing him I was happy and peaceful. I didn't even understand why I felt this way for we had never spoken to one another. But our eyes talked. I soon realized I loved this young man, whose name was Sascha. I knew he loved me, too, for he showed it by the interest he took in my son.

And what our eyes saw, our hearts felt, for it was our love language from the first moment on. I felt no more fear but somehow felt protected by Sascha. "Love overcomes fear" (1 John 4:18). And God's love filters through everywhere.

We had nothing to occupy our time for the Reds had no jobs for us at that time. All we did was to sit idle and feel our empty stomachs aching, for again we were starving. I'd rather take a beating than see my child hungry. It was the worst part of our imprisonment. Of course, the Communists planned to send us to Siberia as soon as possible.

I believe the Lord sent help to Arnold and me through Sascha. He was a good auto mechanic and had volunteered to go to the garage to work on the cars of the KZ camp staff.

Whenever he left, heavy thoughts would fill my hours away from my new-found love. My greatest fear was that we'd be separated and sent to different places in Siberia. My spirit was lifted whenever he'd return to camp, for I could not bear to be separated from him for even a short time.

One day after Sascha had finished working on the cars, the Commander, Colonel Zukov, invited Sascha to his quarters to eat. He had invited him on other occasions as well.

Whenever Colonel Zukov offered him vodka to drink, Sascha refused for he feared it was a trap to make him confess who he was and so on.

One day the Commander gave Sascha a pass to leave the camp and go to the nearby city of Oshatz to buy parts for the car. He told Sascha that if he came back he would personally shoot him on sight. He also told him that that very night transport trains would arrive to move us all out to Siberia. Sascha understood then that this dear Colonel Zukov was giving him an order to escape. Could he trust him or was this a trick? He decided to take the chance, believing Siberia could not be any better than a bullet in the back.

Sascha came to the barracks and slipped a note to me, asking me to take my son and leave immediately but to leave all my belongings behind. I did as he asked without noise or disturbance. Soon he returned with a truck, hid us in the back and headed for the gate of the KZ camp. When the guards asked for a pass we expected the worst, but they did not check under the straw in the truck. They were satisfied when they saw the Colonel's signature. When we heard the gates close behind us, we were elated and relieved for we knew our escape was completely unnoticed. We were afraid to go too far in the truck so we left it behind after about twelve kilometers and took a train, mingling with the Germans who had left their homes to the Czech and Polish governments because of the Yalta agreement. Sudeten-Germans' and East Prussians' territory reverted to the Czech and Polish governments at that time.

The train was traveling toward the British zone and we were to cross the border at Friedland, near Göttingen. At the border the train was unloaded to allow passengers to cross the border by foot. Only those who were ill were brought by bus. By then I was so ill that I could barely stand up. I didn't know what was wrong with me, but everybody else could tell just by looking at me for my skin had turned yellow. So I crossed by bus while Sascha and Arnold crossed by foot where we all arrived safely and were reunited. If I hadn't

been so weak I would have shouted for joy, but I felt joy in
my heart, for once again I was free from Communism!

Chapter 27

MY SECRET EFFORTS REWARDED

In Friedland we had to go through the routine procedure of paper-inspection, disinfection and finally examinations by doctors. When the doctor took a look at me he said, "What's wrong with you? When did you see yourself last?" I said, "Sir, where I come from there were no mirrors." In reply he told me I had yellow jaundice which was highly contagious and that I must go to the hospital for quarantine. Since there was no fight left in me, I agreed to go to the hospital. Sascha and Arnold were taken to a school which had been converted into a refugee camp.

Though we weren't married, I had complete confidence in Sascha's care of Arnold. We had just been reunited at the border and now we were to be separated again. And here I was, exactly two years after arriving in Teplitz-Schesnau from Russia with typhoid fever on Christmas Eve, 1945, going to the hospital. How much had happened in those years!

I spent six weeks in Göttingen Poly-Clinic but was on the road to recovery just two weeks after having been admitted. Arnold, who was now six, came to visit me while Sascha found himself a job. By the time Sascha got to the hospital to pick up Arnold, he was burning up with fever. Two nurses wrapped him in blankets and carried him to the children's ward. Days went by before the tests were returned. Arnold had a hole in one of his lungs and would be in the hospital for several weeks.

We were both released at about the same time. Since we still didn't have a home, the three of us walked to the nearest farming village and found a widow-farmer who gave us three rooms in which to live. Sascha and I were married and finally

Arnold had a father. Arnold and Sascha got along so well that it was a happy time for all of us.

For the first time in years Arnold was able to go to school, while Sascha went to work for the British military government. I helped on the farm and we were rewarded with all the food we needed. Freedom is so wonderful. When one has lived under oppression for so many years, freedom is cherished. In a previous chapter I wrote about how I expected to marry a man from Saxony after my flight from Czechoslovakia. I praise God he did not permit that to happen. Herbert's mother later wrote to tell me that her son had been so brainwashed in a Russian prison that he became a full-fledged Communist. Had I married him, I would have been sent back to Russia because the Russians separated every marriage that took place during the war, by keeping the Germans in Germany and returning the ones born in Russia to Russia. This is another example of God turning a curse into a blessing for me.

Now I began to talk to my husband about my dream to go to America. My hope was high, but he was not ready yet. I had to be patient with him. I believed God would be faithful in bringing us to America, but it would have to be in His own time.

In 1947 I became pregnant again and a daughter, Anastasia, was born. She looked just like her father. But again something went wrong and she died twelve days after she was born. She was baptized and is surely with the Lord in heaven.

Through the Red Cross I found my good friends from Czechoslovakia, Mizzi and Hans Schober. It was perfect timing as they were in a destitute state. Now I could return their many kindnesses to me and my son. When I met them they had only had one daughter named Heidi. But now they had two additional sons as well. They lost all their belongings on their flight to Bavaria near Munich. Their youngest son Peter was born one month after Anastasia died. We had been well provided for by the British government employees at our daughter's birth so now Peter got everything. We loaded a car full of all we had and brought it to them. It was indeed a joyous reunion. After what both families had come through, each of us looked at the other with a deep understanding of the pain suffered by each. They expressed regret for not having listened to my warning about the Communists. Had they heeded my warning, much suffering might have been avoided. Mizzi's brother had been tragically killed while protecting his daughter from rapists while her mother watched them kill her son. As a result, the mother's heart was broken and she remained silent until her death.

After we returned to Göttingen we sent packages and corresponded with the Schobers as often as possible. They had hit it off with Sascha very well so we always enjoyed receiving their letters.

When the change from the Reichsmark (kind of money) to the Deutsche Mark came about, we decided to move to Bavaria, too. It was hard to find work around Munich after the war for everything was in ruins. This proved an advantage in a way, for my husband started to see that he could not make a living for us. It was a struggle and we barely kept our heads above water.

In 1949 another son was born in Munich. We named him Leonard. He was a bundle of joy to all of us. His big brother was especially proud of him. I still had in mind applying for emigration papers for our family of four. I felt it was just a matter of time now before my dream was to be fulfilled.

In 1951 President Truman signed for a new quota of 58,000 Germans born in foreign countries, including Russia. I was sure now was the time. I hurried to fill out an application when I heard the news over the radio. I decided not to tell my husband yet for I was sure he'd say no, but I was determined to get to America. I took my two sons and went to find out about the legalities.

I found out we needed a sponsor who could come through various churches. Inasmuch as we are Catholics, I applied through Saint Rafael's Society, which in turn sent my application to the N.C.W.C. (National Catholic Welfare Conference) who would seek a sponsor for us. Secretly I applied for immigration, hoping my husband would agree. Each time I went alone to the immigration office with my two sons. When a letter would come from them I'd hide it. Every visit to the immigration headquarters would mean waiting in line with many others. We'd all wait in the dusty streets as the long line would move slowly toward the door, into the hallway and then into the office to talk with the persons processing our papers. One was as anxious as the other for a new life in a new country.

When I finally received the long-awaited letter from the C.I.C. (Counterintelligence Corps), I took my sons once again to the office. I was trembling inside for things were really getting serious now, and I knew I'd never get permission for immigration without my husband's signature. As surely as I expected, their first question was, "Where is your husband?" I couldn't say that I had none or that he didn't want to immigrate. Up until now I had proceeded on faith but suddenly I was trembling. I felt like a woman who goes to the airport to take a trip but has no money for the ticket. I was so desperate I told the officer that my husband had a sprained ankle, hoping to buy time.

The very next day a tall, good-looking officer came into our yard. He was from South Carolina in the United States. He saw my husband walking around as well as usual. I was so ashamed for fibbing; I thought I'd sink into the ground. I never dreamed an officer would come to our house before Sascha's "sprained ankle" had a chance to heal. I discovered right there and then that honesty was the best policy. This was not Russia, where one dared not always speak the truth.

The officer caught on quickly to what was happening so I told him the truth. I now had more time to explain than I had in the office, and he proved to be most understanding. He was a perfect southern gentleman.

He accomplished more than I ever could have by talking

to my husband. He painted a beautiful picture of the United States and explained how our going there would be good for our children. He said we'd be much better off in America. Besides, Germany was not our birthplace nor our real home. The two men got along very well, and before the C.I.C. officer left he had my husband's signature. From then on we made our plans together and talked at great lengths about the United States. I promised myself at that time to never undertake such a task by myself again.

Our papers passed through all the necessary channels and we were notified to report for physicals at the immigration camp. Of all the camps where we had been throughout the war and post-war years, this was the most joyous of all. X-rays were taken and we were given all the injections necessary for departure. In spite of my fears there wasn't a trace of scar tissue left on my lungs as a result of the sickness I had had in Czechoslovakia. We all passed with flying colors.

We met many good friends in this camp and exchanged addresses so we could write and visit one another in America. We became close to one couple in particular, Walter and Irene Donner. They were immigrating to Springfield, Massachusetts so we took their address along with many others. They left before we did since they were going to the North and landing in New York. Our sponsor was from California so we waited for a boat to take us to New Orleans.

We left by train for Bremerhoven. Upon arriving at the port we boarded the military ammunitions ship, "The General Sturges." At last I was on the last step of the long journey of my dreams, and visions of a new life of freedom in the land I had heard about since childhood would soon be fulfilled. In a sense, I was finally going home!

Chapter 28

THE MIRACLE THAT SET ME REALLY FREE

And so here I was with Sascha, Lennie and Arnold seeing my new home for the first time. How I marveled at the wonder of this glorious land! In the train I ran from one window to another and could not sit still. I was so like a little child that men and women on the train could not help but smile. I was like a lark set free to investigate new vistas. Arnold and Sascha sat quietly but Lennie and I hopped and bobbed and giggled and grinned. Oh, such joy to see such plenty, such abundance, such majesty, such beauty! I shall never forget that train ride for it was a highpoint in my life.

We were met at Grand Central Station by two men from the N.C.W.C. office on Madison Avenue in New York. We took a taxi to their office in order to fill out more papers and discuss our chances for a new sponsor. After that interview the men took us to a hotel near Second Avenue where we could rest and await further instructions.

The next morning Sascha and I went out with the boys to look at the nearby stores. We were so anxious to investigate our new country. We found a small Jewish grocery store on Second Avenue and went in to purchase food. The owner spoke Russian so we really were thrilled for the opportunity to ask questions. And did I ask questions! I showed him the addresses that we had received from the people in the immigration camp in Germany and asked him where these places were. The Jewish man got a map of the United States and began to search for these places. The first place we looked for was Springfield, Massachusetts for that was the destination of the Donners. When we found out it was only a few hours away, we truly rejoiced.

Sascha and I returned to the hotel with our boys and anxiously awaited a phone call from the N.C.W.C. office. We didn't have to wait long before they called to see how we were getting along. That's when I told them about our friends, the Donners. They contacted them for us through the placement office in Springfield. The Donners, in turn, arranged for a sponsor for us from Springfield. And so off we went again by train to Massachusetts.

We settled in Springfield and Sascha got a job right away. After we were somewhat settled I, too, started to work. Lennie was sent to nursery school and Arnold started school. He learned English in three weeks, but Lennie was young and didn't enjoy being left alone each day. Arnold helped me learn English at first and then I began to learn it from others at work. Within three years we purchased our own home.

I walked through the aisles of supermarkets or clothing stores and felt I was living in a fairy tale, seeing all the wondrous plenty before me. I still get excited when I think how fortunate we are in this free land of bounty. Yet I shall never waste anything nor forget those lean years. I will never forget what it is like to be hungry, and I feel for those in the world who are starving. I got my white dress, shoes, hat and gloves and, yes, even the elegant car I dreamed of in the Ukraine.

But after several years the initial excitement wore off and emptiness began to set in. Later, depression hung over me like a cloud. All my joy seemed to vanish and I became sad and melancholy. I was unable to adjust to such a good life knowing my sisters, brother and parents were in Siberia cold and hungry, if still alive at all. If I could only let them know that I was really in America! If I could only say, "Thank you" to my Dad for kindling the fire in my heart! If only I could say, "I made it, Dad, in spite of all the obstacles!" But I could not.

Then guilt set in. I'd say to myself, "Why me? Why did I escape while millions of people better than I died in Siberia?" I thought of my little sisters who had not even lived yet. They were like angels to me. But in myself I could see nothing good at all. My mind was tormented. I began to wish I had died. I began to question God: "Why did You save a wreck like me? Why didn't You let me die?"

I went on and on torturing myself. I'd go to doctors. I went to one psychiatrist after another. I used all the medication available and yet I did not get better. I'd come out of the dark clouds once in a while, but then I'd go right back to the darkness because it seemed safer somehow. My doctor tagged it "circumstantial depression." It didn't matter to me what he called it. All I knew then was that I was terribly unhappy. My drive in life had absolutely disappeared. My poor husband and sons couldn't believe it was me. I put them through a lot during that time for they could not understand what was wrong.

Physically I was perfectly healthy. I'd go to church and pray, but there would be no change. I went on like this for eight years until one Sunday afternoon in 1960 a tremendous restlessness filled my being and I just couldn't sit still. I wandered from room to room. I'd turn the TV on and then turn it off. I took books off the shelf only to put them down after reading one paragraph. It was terrible!

For the third time I turned the TV on and tuned to a station I usually didn't get, Channel 18 out of Hartford, Connecticut. The Oral Roberts Healing Crusade was on. I immediately settled down. I was very interested. I was all ears and hung on to every word, every prayer. I was so disappointed when the program was over, for I could have stayed glued to the set all day. At the end Oral Roberts pointed his finger at me and said, "God bless you and read your Bible!" It was like a command from God and not Oral Roberts. I obeyed instantly. I found the large Bible my sons had given me on Christmas Eve two years before, took it out of the box from which I had never removed it and began to read. I could not stop for anything. I was annoyed when I had to do housework or prepare meals. I read through the Gospels, the Book of Acts, the whole New Testament, in fact. Now I knew what was missing in my life.

I talked continuously now with the Lord. No matter what I would do—cleaning, cooking, driving—I carried on this conversation with Jesus. One day, soon after I finished reading my Bible, I was ironing and again I was talking with the Lord and reminiscing about my whole life. Suddenly a holy sorrow overcame me for all my sins. I was convicted by the Holy Spirit. I fell on my knees and through my many tears confessed all my sins. As I wept and spluttered my sins out to God, it seemed like concrete walls broke away from my innermost being. I felt as though hot water were rushing through me, cleansing me until I felt clean as a new-born baby. I didn't know what was happening to me except that it was beautiful, wonderful, glorious and I never wanted whatever it was to leave me. I felt the Lord's presence in such a way that if I had reached out I would have touched Him. And so I met my Lord in a beautiful, unforgettable way.

But I had no Christian friends to turn to. I found no one who understood what I was talking about. So perhaps a year later I slipped right back into depression, which went on until 1972 when the psychiatrist finally decided to give me shock treatments. I didn't care at the time for I wanted to be well at all costs, or die. I had eight shock treatments but to no avail for I was worse than ever. I felt as if I lived in complete darkness and despair.

In 1973 I was invited to Oral Roberts University to attend a seminar on the Holy Spirit. I went, hoping I'd have another experience as in 1960, but nothing exciting like that happened again. I was prayed over for the baptism in the Holy Spirit but felt no different after they prayed.

I had been desperately looking for an experience, but instead God quietly blessed me. After returning home I began to desire to praise the Lord everywhere—at work, driving, at home. The gifts of the Holy Spirit began to operate in me. One day at work the Lord clearly spoke to me about going to a prayer meeting. I couldn't believe there was such a thing as a prayer meeting in our area, but after many inquiries I found one. It really helped to find brothers and sisters with whom to share. They prayed with and for me about my problem.

Then one Sunday morning the breakthrough finally came. My son Lenny was mowing the lawn and I was raking the grass when all of a sudden the Lord spoke to me again. He said, "You have not because you ask not." Without realizing it I asked, "Then why am I here and my sisters and parents are in Siberia?" Immediately He replied, "Because they never asked to come to the United States but you did. Remember when you were six years old?"

Now I understood that God is a faithful God. In spite of my many sins, He brought me through it all. He knew all along that He could deal with me, a sinner, after I was here in the safety of His harbor, the United States of America.

"When all was dark and night,
And I was sick to die;
My Jesus came to me
And made me whole.
He healed my broken heart,
And wiped my tears away.

He took my hand in His
And began to lead the way.
I gave my heart to Him;
He gave His life for me.
He took my grief and strife;
He wants but all my life.

He opened prison gates
And set the captive free.
He made the lame to walk,
And caused the blind to see.
My Jesus does all this
For you and me.

And when I hear the spoken word,
"This is my body
Take, eat and behold,"
Then my Jesus whispers to me,
"It was worth it all."

97

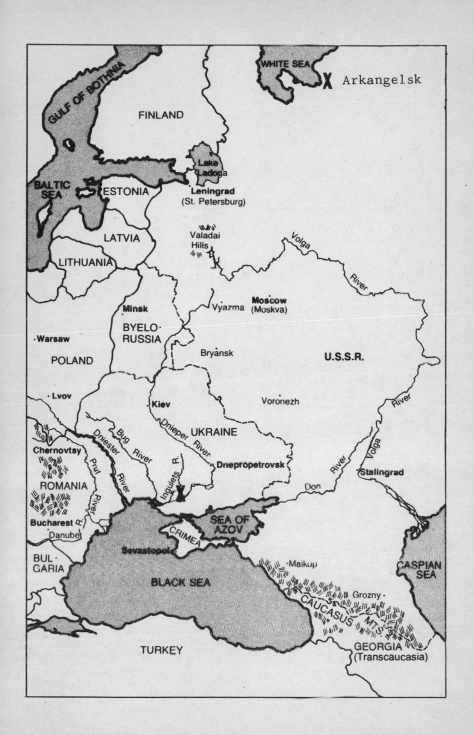

It Was Worth It All

Words and Music by
ELLY MATZ
Arr. by Dorothy Buss

When all was dark as night And I was sick to die, My
(He) wants my grief and strife He wants but all my life, I

Je - sus came to me —— He came to make me whole.—— He healed my bro - ken
gave my heart to Him —— He gave His life for me.—— He o - pened pris - on

heart And wiped my tears a - way, —— He took my hand in His And be -
gates And set the cap - tive free, —— He made the lame to walk And

gan to lead the way. He
caused the blind to see. My Je - sus the hope for

you and me. And when I hear the spo - ken word, this is my bod - y

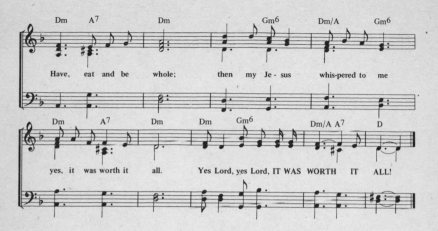

Have, eat and be whole; then my Je - sus whis-pered to me

yes, it was worth it all. Yes Lord, yes Lord, IT WAS WORTH IT ALL!

I Gave My Heart to Jesus

I gave my heart to Je - sus I gave my heart to Him__ Who sweat for me, Who
I gave my heart to Je - sus I gave my heart to Him__ Who watched o'er me and
I gave my heart to Je - sus I gave my heart to Him__ whom I love,

bled for me, Who car-ried for all sweet vic - to - ry. I gave my heart to Je - sus, I
guard-ed me, Who won sweet vic - to - ry for all.
Whom I praise, to Him be-long-ing all my days.

Chorus

gave my heart to Him; Who died for me and set me free from all my sin and slav-er-y.

MEAL FROM THE MILL—*by Berla Yoder.* . . . .*$.95*
A clever book of proverbs for today by a modern Solomon.

THE GREATNESS OF GOD—*by Earl Bergman.* *$1.95*
A dynamic and soul-stirring portrayal of God the Father. Everyone needs to read it.

TREASURES IN SONG—*by Gwen Shaw and Dorothy Buss* *$3.50*
A wonderful book of songs! Many given by inspiration of the Holy Spirit to Sister Gwen while on the mission field. Includes the story behind each song.

Order your copies from:

    END-TIME HANDMAIDENS, P. O. Box 447, Jasper, ARK 72641

If you would like more information about this missionary organization and would like to receive our timely and informative news publications free, write to:

END-TIME HANDMAIDENS, P.O. Box 447, Jasper, ARK 72641.

NAME _____

STREET _____

CITY _____ STATE _____ ZIP _____

Quantity	Title	Price

Postage & Handling add 5% (55¢ minimum) _____

                                              TOTAL _____

READ

The prophecies, which were given to Mother Barbara concerning the nations in our time.

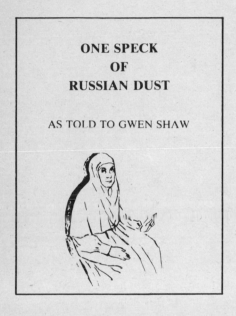

ONE SPECK
OF
RUSSIAN DUST

AS TOLD TO GWEN SHAW

$1.30 (postage paid)

When the End-Time Handmaidens visited Israel in September 1978, Sister Gwen had a personal visit with one of the greatest women of our time. She feels led to share this experience with you. You will never be the same after reading the thrilling testimony of Abbess Mother Barbara, Mount of Olives, Jerusalem. The prophecies, which were given to her concerning the nations of the world in our time by a holy bishop of the Kremlin ten days before his death, will startle you and prove to you how close we are to the end time.